Soil and Survival

Soil and Survival

LAND STEWARDSHIP AND THE FUTURE OF AMERICAN AGRICULTURE

Joe Paddock
Nancy Paddock
Carol Bly

Sierra Club Books San Francisco

The Sierra Club, founded in 1892 by John Muir, has devoted itself to the study and protection of the earth's scenic and ecological resources—mountains, wetlands, woodlands, wild shores and rivers, deserts and plains. The publishing program of the Sierra Club offers books to the public as a nonprofit educational service in the hope that they may enlarge the public's understanding of the Club's basic concerns. The point of view expressed in each book, however, does not necessarily represent that of the Club. The Sierra Club has some sixty chapters coast to coast, in Canada, Hawaii, and Alaska. For information about how you may participate in its programs to preserve wilderness and the quality of life, please address inquiries to Sierra Club, 730 Polk Street, San Francisco, CA 94109.

Sierra Club Books paperback edition: 1988

Chapters 1, 2, 3, 4, 6, 7, 10, 13, and 14 written by Joe Paddock. Chapters 8, 9, and 11 written by Nancy Paddock. Chapter 12 compiled and edited by Nancy Paddock. Chapter 15 written by Joe Paddock and Nancy Paddock. Chapter 5 written by Carol Bly.

The publisher gratefully acknowledges permission to reprint copyrighted text from *Book of the Hopi*, by Frank Waters (copyright © 1963 by Frank Waters. Reprinted by permission of Viking Penguin, Inc.); from *Circles on the Water*, by Marge Piercy (copyright © by Alfred A. Knopf, Inc.); and from *Green Paradise Lost*, by Elizabeth Dodson Gray (copyright © 1979, 1981 by Elizabeth Dodson Gray. Reprinted by permission of Roundtable Press.)

LIBRARY OF CONGRESS CATALOGING IN PUBLICATION DATA
Paddock, Joe.
Soil and survival.
Includes index.
1. Land use, Rural—Government policy—United States.
2. Soil conservation—Government policy—United States.
3. Agricultural conservation—Government policy—United States. 4. Food supply—Government policy—United States. I. Paddock, Nancy. II. Bly, Carol. III. Title.
HD256.P32 1986 333.76'0973 86-3988
ISBN 0-87156-725-3

Cover design by Paul Bacon
Book design by Abigail Johnston

Printed in the United States of America

10 9 8 7 6 5 4 3 2 1

This book is dedicated to Ron Kroese,
director of the Land Stewardship Project,
who over the years, with sensitivity and generosity,
supported us through each phase of its development.

Acknowledgments

We wish to thank the Minnesota Humanities Commission for financial support in the early development of some of the content of this book that was used as educational material by the Land Stewardship Project.

We wish also to thank Cathy Simon and Lou Kromrey for secretarial help; and Victor Ray, Doug Nopar, Mary Turck, and other kind friends for reading and criticizing portions of the manuscript.

Contents

INTRODUCTION

EVERY ton of topsoil slipping seaward from its hillside home, beyond natural replacement levels, represents a failure of culture. Soil erosion is not a simple matter of poor practice or lapsed memory or bad luck due to an unlikely rain. It is the failure of us as a people to comprehend that we have yet to discover America, that we have only colonized it. Because we are a fallen species, and by this I mean a species out of context with the nature that spawned us, we are now forced into being participants in the Creation in a manner unprecedented by any other species probably in this part of our sidereal universe. Though the chance to be a participant in the Creation may be in the category of adventure, it is a frightening adventure, for we could fail. For openers, we may not have the ethical stretch in this paleolithic being of ours. We may not have the staying power. We could even get tired before we really begin. The poet Gary Snyder says that it is a 2,000 year journey before us. It *is* a journey that will require poets and stonemasons, musicians and farmers, artists and even scientists. As the last of the fossil fuel reserves wink out, and the Faustian bargain of nuclear power is more evenly comprehended across the population, we will have to give soil its due. On a global basis, we have squandered more soil carbon than the fossil variety. Roughly a third of our soil carbon was lost with the opening up of the North American continent.

Here is a book that will help us in that long stretch before us. This is not one more "ain't it awful" book. It is a book written by two poets and an essayist and fiction writer who have worked together on farmland issues for eight years. Pay no attention to the cynic's sneers that myth and songs cannot stop sheet erosion. Just remember that the single vision of hardheaded science and technology has been used to accelerate the loss of useful atoms from our nation's slopes. And remember, too, that the National Soil Loss Equation does not measure the indignity of a future with more potbellied children, more children who will never learn to read. That equation measures "acceptable loss."

This is more than a book about soil and survival. The authors have been much too modest in their title selection. This is a book about soil and life, soil and our roots, soil and culture, soil and civilization. As far back as 1940, E. B. White could "see no reason for a conservation program if people have lost their knack with the earth." White could see "no reason for saving the streams to make the power to run the factories if the resultant industry reduces the status and destroys the heart of the individual." He called this the most "frightful sort of dissipation." White saw the necessary connections, yet in the nearly half century that has passed since he wrote those words, nearly all of our efforts at protecting soil and water have ignored this dimension and we have failed miserably.

Here is a book then which seeks to make that connection, which seeks to help us all establish that "knack with the earth." What we should have learned in the half century since the Soil Conservation Service was formed is that protection of our soil and water is not an engineering problem alone. To simply give water advice with terraces and grass waterways is an inadequate engineering trick. Applying biological methods on the farm alone won't do either. To the entire array of efforts already tried individually and together we now know that we must add the thoughts of those who have studied and listened to the human heart. We must add the missing content that, as Aldo Leopold said, will "change our loyalties and affections."

One warning. This "knack with the earth" business is not to be treated as a *piece* of the pie which includes all of the sound engineering methods and biological controls. It is the *source* from which all things flow. The proper implementation of technique is a *derivative* of that source, that "knack." These authors deal with that "knack." In my experience there has never been another book quite like this. Here it is.

Wes Jackson
Salina, Kansas
February 12, 1986

· I ·

Inside The Land Organism

· 1 ·

Prologue:

SOMETHING WE CAN CHANGE

> "I got to figure," the tenant said. "We all got to figure. There's some way to stop this. It's not like lightning or earthquakes. We've got a bad thing made by men, and by God that's something we can change."
>
> John Steinbeck
> *The Grapes of Wrath*

DURING that immense reach of time since planetary life first sparked and began its struggle, a thin layer of topsoil has developed over those areas most hospitable to the creatures that thrive and multiply on this earth. Considering the aeons of struggle and the price in lives, this layer of topsoil is almost unimaginably thin: a few inches, a foot, rarely two. It is the end product of all the life that has ever gone on in this place we call Earth. It is the magical medium through which old age and disease are transformed again and again into fresh and vital new life. It is the stuff of our flesh and our future. We, earth's creatures, are but a haze that rises above this substance—always returning, always rising again.

About ten thousand years back, humankind learned to cultivate this thin layer of stored energy, stored life. Defying the interlocking protective systems that held the thin layer in place throughout the ages, agriculture began. At first this was of small import, but as humankind multiplied and spread over almost every habitable region of the globe, the toll mounted. In time, it could be said that nothing had changed the surface of the earth so much as agriculture. The green dawn of our beginnings, alive with birdsong and bright dew, has passed on now to a darker afternoon.

The Global 2000 Report to the President tells us that we have probably missed the opportunity to stabilize the earth's population at ten billion.[1] Are we truly heading for such density? There seems to be agreement that we are. If so, those children born on this morning will see things we can scarcely imagine. Even now, in a world that still produces food in plenty, many millions are malnourished, even starving. Watching numbly before TV screens, we see gaunt men and women of the sub-Sahara sitting at road's edge, waiting for food that all too often does not arrive. We hear a translator tell a mother's tale of an immense journey on foot, through the sands of an advancing desert, in search of food. Before our very eyes, swollen-bellied children seem already to be merging with the dust. All lives are a journey toward dust, but need they end so soon?

It is possible, even likely, that by the time you read this, rain will have fallen in the sub-Sahara, and the ancient exchange between these suffering people and their soil will have been resumed, though at a diminished level. Life, moving to the ancient rhythms, will perhaps be good again. But many see this current crisis as a warning, believe that the stage is now set for a succession of such tragedies.

Much of the world's best farmland is now threatened because our species lacks commitment to a spiritual and ethical vision of our interconnectedness with the land. Farmland is primary human habitat, and black winds, dark rivers are carrying it away. Our good health, the smiles on the faces of our grandchildren are being carried to places beyond our reach.

In the United States and around the globe, farmland protection has emerged as the major land-use issue of the 1980s. Analysts such as Lester R. Brown and Edward C. Wolf of the Worldwatch Institute warn us about this enormous and growing problem. This book is inspired by the belief that, barring nuclear disaster, erosion is the most certain threat to the long-term future of civilization. The response to this threat, in the United

States and virtually everywhere else, has been weak and uncoordinated.

Our cultural memory is too short. Apparently we cannot learn from the lessons that etched the lives of our forebears. It seems we must suffer the same pains in our own flesh, in our own psyches, before the lessons take. There are many alive in the United States today who experienced the great mid-continental dust storms of the thirties, a decade they remember as the "dirty thirties." Yet after one generation of serious conservation effort, levels of erosion have risen again to those of the Dust Bowl days. I have talked to many men and women who experienced those early dust storms, and they described them as awful—with an emphasis on the *aw(e)*:

"Out in the field, why, when she'd hit—and she'd come on *fast*!—you'd have to get a bandana over your mouth and nose or you'd choke up on it. Be like drowning in dust."

"Your horses would kind of snort and squeal, twisting in their harness, but they couldn't get away from it."

"So dark the chickens would go to roost in midday."[2]

Chickens to roost in midday! The cosmic clock gone awry. People said, "You wondered if it was the end of the world." Many still believe, grasping a greater time span, that such moments in the history of our species are the beginning of an ending. As we have been suggesting, a major farmland crisis may be less than a millennium away. Since the middle of our century, world population—and demands for food—have doubled. We have moved into exponential rates of population growth. By century's end, world population is expected to be half again what it was in the early eighties. The connection between such population growth and our planet's farmland is clear.

Worldwatch Institute, an organization created to analyze and focus attention on global problems, deals with the quiet crisis of soil erosion on our planet. In *Worldwatch Paper 60,* Lester R. Brown and Edward C. Wolf point out that steadily increasing erosion is due not to diminished skills on the part of farmers, but to an expanding demand for food. In response, the world's food producers have increasingly plowed hilly and otherwise fragile lands that erode very easily. Little by little they have abandoned the rotations whereby one year's crop helps to replace what has been taken from the soil by the preceding one. Instead, they have monocropped, planting the same cash-producing crop in the same field year after year, masking losses in fertility by using more and more chemical fertilizer. Almost always the single crop planted is a row crop, such as corn or soybeans, which exposes the soil to the ravages of wind and rain far more than do densely planted crops, such as alfalfa or wheat. Using land more intensively implies a need for a corresponding increase in conservation efforts, but in most cases the farmer actually has *less* time, energy, and resources to devote to conservation than before.

It is difficult to visualize the enormous amount of topsoil that is lost to erosion. We need it pictured for us. In 1950, when annual soil loss in the United States was less than it is now, J. Russell Smith, in his book *Tree Crops,* wrote: "The U.S. Soil Conservation Service reports that the soil washed out and blown out of the fields of the United States each year would load a modern freight train long enough to reach around the world eighteen times."[3] Not once, but every year, year in and year out.

Natural processes do replace topsoil, usually at a rate of between one and five tons per acre each year. Therefore the authors of *Worldwatch Paper 60* prefer to talk, not of gross losses in topsoil, but of the amounts lost above and beyond what is replaced. From this perspective, the yearly net loss in the United States is 1.7 billion tons. Large as this figure is, it is the smallest loss in any of the world's four leading food-producing nations. Of the other three, according to best available information, the Soviet Union has net erosion amounting to 2.5 billion tons per year, China 4.3 billion, and India 4.7 billion. These four countries hold 52 percent of the world's farmland and produce more than half its food.[4]

Brown and Wolf report that by taking air samples, scientists in Hawaii can tell when spring plowing has begun in northern China. Elsewhere, extremely heavy sediment loads reveal that the Yellow River of China and the sacred Ganges of India are carrying away the future of those who live in their drainage basins. So, too, the Volga and the Mississippi.

In almost every other country in the world, the situation is at least as bad. In *Worldwatch Paper 60,* we read of an "ecological emergency in Java," an "ecological nightmare" unfolding in Ethiopia's highlands, "desert-like conditions caused by wind erosion" spreading in Bolivia, and a recent doubling of "abandoned cultivated land" in Iran. For the planet as a whole the estimated net yearly loss of topsoil to erosion is an incomprehensible 25.4 billion tons.[5] Again, not once, but every year, year in and year out. Those who say such a statistic does not represent a clear and present crisis must be very short-sighted indeed.

In only one Third World country, Kenya, do the Worldwatch authors find a model for hope. With the help of Swedish geographer and soil specialist Carl-Gösta Wenner, Kenya has developed an effective approach to soil conservation that recognizes the country's traditional form of agriculture and depends upon the committed involvement of peasant farmers.[6] Other nations that manage to care for their land are small countries such as Holland and Japan with well-knit cultures and a strong sense of how sacred, and limited, is their land. Holland, indeed, has had to wrest much of its land from the sea, surely a good prelude to stewardship. By stewardship here we mean an approach to land use that recognizes we are not absolute owners, but caretakers of a portion of creation that should not be diminished during our tenure.

We in the United States have been enormously blessed with farmland. Only about 11 percent of the surface of the earth is high-quality farmland, and at least one-eighth of this exists within our borders. Such a blessing implies an equally large responsibility, but, as we have seen, the degradation of our farmland base is very considerable.

The greatest concentration of prime farmland in the United States—and perhaps in the world—exists in the state of Iowa. After one century of agricultural activity, the topsoil of Iowa is half gone.[7] A frequently quoted graphic description of soil loss tells us that an Iowa farmer, on the average, loses two bushels of topsoil for every bushel of corn grown.[8] Some say the loss is really much higher. Certainly it is higher in the case of soybeans, Iowa's other major crop. Farmland in the state of Iowa as a whole suffers an average soil loss of just under ten tons per acre per year. In deep loess hill regions losses average just under sixteen tons. In certain local areas losses go much higher. Soil losses in other states of the American breadbasket, though not quite so high, are similar to those of Iowa.[9]

What has gone wrong? For one thing, our enormous blessing in land has led to complacency. For another, fluctuating political and economic conditions have made our farmers more attentive to preserving their way of life than to preserving their soil. Then, too, national policy makers have seen agricultural production and export as one of very few ways by which we might resist an unhealthy international balance of trade. Some say we export soil in exchange for oil, swap topsoil for Toyotas.

To capitalize on our agricultural prowess, in the early seventies, Agriculture Secretary Earl Butz issued his famous call for farmers to "plant fencerow to fencerow" and triggered a great new plow-out of our more fragile lands. Overproduction and glutted markets (aggravated by boycotts) proved Butz's call to be at least premature, but the resulting increase in soil erosion is still with us. Our farmers, meanwhile, in order to survive *individually* within poor market conditions, struggle to produce more and more, thereby aggravating both the problems of overproduction and of erosion.

Erosion is not the only way we lose farmland. Others are desertification, salinization, and diminished fertility. Chemical approaches to farming greatly reduce soil life and humus content, and thus fertility. Such losses in organic content also make soils more easily erodible. Most agricultural experts argue that meeting world food demands would be impossible without the use of agricultural chemicals, yet these diminutions in soil quality are already making themselves felt. Ever more chemical fertilizer is needed to maintain peak yields. Many farmers complain of a chalky deadness in their soils.

In the United States, as much land is lost to development as to erosion. Housing projects, roads and highways (including our vast interstate system), shopping malls, airports, athletic facilities, power plants, water impoundments, strip mines—these all take enormous bites from our farmland base. The deep and level soils of prime farmland have always been the easiest on which to develop. Many of our towns, large and small, were established on a rich agricultural plain, and it is now common to see "belts of newness" surrounding them. It is much more convenient to place a tract of houses on such land than, say, on a nearby stretch of rocky hills, and we are doing so apace. In a 1981 guidebook, the National Agricultural Lands Study describes the magnitude of farmland lost to development: "Visualize a strip of land half a mile wide stretching from New York to California. That is one million acres—the amount of important farmland converted to other uses and irreversibly lost to agriculture every year in the United States."[10]

The American Farmland Trust estimates that anywhere from one-third to one-half of this is prime farmland. How much food might this have provided for how many hungry people? And the loss is permanent. The situation in the rest of the world is much the same:

> In the industrialized countries . . . the amount of land devoted to urban uses has been increasing twice as fast as population. The limited data available for less developed countries point to similar trends. In Egypt, for example, despite efforts to open new lands to agriculture, the total area of irrigated farmland has remained almost unchanged in the past two decades. As fast as additional acres are irrigated with water from the Aswan Dam, old producing lands on the Nile are converted to urban uses.[11]

But enough of this listing of loss. During and after the Dust Bowl, many in the United States felt those ravages to the land in their own flesh. They were in agreement with the Wintu Indian woman who asked, "How can the spirit of the earth like the white man? . . . Everywhere the white man has touched, it is sore."[12] Much of this pain has been inflicted in the name of agriculture, and since the retreat of the last glacier, as has been said, perhaps nothing has changed the surface of the earth so much as agriculture.

Many who felt the pain tried to do something about it, and we have in the history of soil conservation in the United States at least one story of the right man being in the right place at the right time. The man was Hugh Hammond Bennett. He began his career in 1902 as a young scientist classifying and mapping soils in the southeastern United States. In 1928, before the Soil Conservation Service had yet been conceived, his publication "Soil Erosion—A National Menace" helped to awaken interest in the growing problem. Within a few years, the realities of the "dirty thirties" had become undeniable, and in 1935, the Soil Erosion Service (which in time became the Soil Conservation Service) began, with Hugh Bennett as its chief.

Under Bennett the SES approached soil conservation in four ways: through science, through farmer participation, through publicity, and through congressional relations. Bennett was a powerful and charismatic figure who, for a time, managed to pull together an impressive organization. Occasionally, he also had some luck:

> The second major dust storm on March 6, 1935, was tracked by SES personnel, who reported to Bennett as it moved across the country, from fields in the southern Great Plains and into Washington, D. C. The day it arrived in Washington, D. C., Bennett was working with congressmen in their offices. He told them the dust storm was coming—most were skeptical—and about when the dust would start sifting onto their desks. He was right—it happened almost precisely as he predicted. Needless to say, the stature of Bennett and his soil conservation cause were greatly enhanced throughout the halls of Congress.[13]

At his retirement, in 1952, Bennett could claim that more than 1.3 billion acres were enrolled in the SCS program and that nearly five million farms—more than double the number of farms that now *exist* in the United States—were in some way cooperating.[14] Bennett was obviously one individual who, working with many other gifted individuals, made a difference.

Since Bennett's time, the soil conservation movement in the United States has waned, and the push for agricultural production has greatly increased. In real terms, considerably more was spent on conservation in the United States in the late 1940s than is spent now. With the focus on erosion-producing row crops during the seventies, topsoil losses rival those of the thirties.

The 1985 Farm Bill does contain interesting new conservation legislation. Its intent is to keep highly erosive marginal lands out of production. For one thing, it will pay farmers to retire some of our problem land. Over the next five years as much as 50 million acres could be put into a conservation reserve. 1985 legislation will also deny farm program benefits to those who bring *new* marginal land into production. After 1990, this new legislation will deny farm program benefits to those who do not employ conservation practices on highly erodible lands. Farmers affected by this law will have until 1995 to achieve full compliance.

There are some who call this new legislation historic. They might be right. Its focus on problem land is highly commendable, but I suggest that we be very cautious in our enthusiasm. Congressional commitment to long-term funding of the reserve program seems weak. In that this is a voluntary program, the fact that farmers have been slow to sign up for it also adds an element of doubt as to its future. Most believe that quality of implementation will be the key to the success of the new legislation, and all too often conservation programs have failed for lack of such committed effort. That which has proven profitable to farmers has succeeded. The rest, however useful for preserving farmland, has tended to fall by the way.

What is most troubling about the new legislation is that many legislators see it, not as an addition to old programs, but as a lower cost substitute for them. In fact, it seems that our present administration in 1986 would, if given a free hand, dissolve the Soil Conservation Service which Hugh Bennett fathered. Some are saying that its operating budget will soon be reduced by from 30 to 50 percent.

There are those who are bitter about how, through the seventies and early eighties, we drifted away from our previously serious conservation effort. As an elderly farmer from the Red River Valley of western Minnesota said at a land stewardship meeting, "It's like we're having to start all over again from scratch." His heavy hands worked in his lap. "It's as if none of it meant anything. We're right back where we started from."

On the same day, about a hundred miles west in North Dakota, I listened to another lament, that of a young district conservationist for the SCS. Cutbacks in budget had left him entirely alone in his district, without even adequate secretarial help. He had responsibilities for many thousands of acres of prime farmland, and it was taking most of his time just to run the office. How was he to get out into the field to aid farmers with conservation planning? How was he to fulfill his educative function within his community? And he was looking at even deeper cutbacks in his budget for the coming year. He understood that he soon might even be expected to take a "furlough" without pay. This young man came from the sort of farm background that emphasizes doing a job well, and the shame and outrage caused by his current plight showed in his face.

"I'm looking," he told me, "I'm looking for a new job." And we and the land, I fear, are going to be losing.

The authors of *Worldwatch Paper 60* point out that our SCS, in 1982, completed an exhaustive survey of U.S. soil conditions. Such a survey, unique among the major food-producing nations, provides the information to enable us to launch an effective soil protection program that would be a model for the world. Unfortunately, to this point, for lack of leadership, we have failed to do so.

Those who believe that federal government should not be involved in soil conservation should, this very moment, begin to consider how this task can be accomplished through local government or the private sector. Let us not, in the meantime, dismantle the system we have. If the men and women of our Soil Conservation Service have in any way failed, it is because we as a nation have displayed only token concern with the problem. Soil conservation has not been mandatory. If, in fact, all farmers had voluntarily come to the SCS to implement full conservation plans on their land, budget and personnel could have aided only a small percentage of them. Obviously we were never serious about ending soil loss in the United States, and it must be admitted that too many farm operators are relieved when they don't have to make that effort.

A few years back an editorial written in the *Des Moines Register* set the cost of correcting the nation's soil conservation problems at about ten billion dollars. What might the figure be now? What will it be ten years from now? It may be, however, that dollar amounts are *not* the critical issue here, that the bottom line is not the "bottom line" in soil conservation. It is this writer's belief that when we have collectively achieved the proper attitude and commitment, the necessary money will be forthcoming. It was, after all, not during good times, but during the Great Depression, that the Soil Erosion Service was first funded by Congress.

The authors of this book work with the St. Paul–based Land Stewardship Project. Among other things, this project holds grassroots land stewardship meetings in SCS-targeted high-erosion counties in a five-state area of the upper Midwest. Our approach, as might be expected, is values-oriented, and project experience is the matrix from which much of this book has emerged.

All too often, those who speak with greatest conviction at land stewardship meetings, sad to say, claim: "It comes down to the bottom line. If the farmer has enough money to care for his land, he will, and if he doesn't, he won't." This statement we call a wipeout. It is based in a desire to avoid the real stewardship issues. If accepted, it is death to all positive effort, and I have seen groups that would not be budged beyond it. But it just isn't true! Financial conditions are absolutely basic to proper care of farmland, but it cannot be assumed that upswings in farm prosperity will automatically lead to greater conservation efforts. In fact, more often than not, farmers have invested increased income into farming even more intensively, to the *detriment* of their land, instead of taking better care of it.

At a certain level of insight our relationship to land comes clear in the mind. We then know our connectedness—and indebtedness—in our bones; our ethical responsibility to the land then moves beyond the level of abstract idea to become a deep, emotionally based imperative. That is what land stewardship is about. At this point, an individual or a population group truly begins to care for land. Not before.

Another more subtle financial "wipeout argument" runs this way: "Economic factors led us into this situation, and economic factors will lead us out." The logic here is that farmers will soon move into various forms of reduced or "conservation" tillage because such practices lower the costs of farming. Or that they will learn to use lesser amounts of chemicals as their costs increase. For whatever reason, there are those who desperately want to reduce the world to the black-and-white simplicity of the balance sheet. Perhaps this is a way of avoiding the feeling side of one's nature. Why else might the former director of the U.S. Office of Management and Budget describe family farm foreclosures as a sign of a dynamic economy?

A few days after hearing David Stockman's comment beamed to a TV audience of millions, I sat in an audience of sixteen while a young dairy farmer from Holland, Sjoerd de Hoop, questioned certain premises at the heart of American agriculture. He was profoundly troubled by wind erosion he'd seen on fields in western Minnesota a few days before. He quoted a fellow farmer from Holland:

"How can they [U.S. farmers] farm and care for their land without . . . continuity? How can you farm when you can't count on conditions, your farm program, to be stable for even a few months?" Speaking for himself, de Hoop continued, "When I heard that your president wants, in one stroke, to cut the U.S. agricultural budget by so many billions of dollars, I thought it was some kind of a joke."

Yes, our farm community is a victim of uncertainty. This group upon which we all depend for our very sustenance should be able to live on and with their land, as if it were their life work, not merely an investment activity to be dropped at the first downturn as implied by Mr. Stockman's statement. Those countries that have, in the past, experienced hunger—whether the reason was war, drought, or diminished farmland—go to great lengths to see that those who produce their food are in a stable condition, so they may plan with the long-term well-being of their land in mind. Holland, as de Hoop implied, has, through government support and regulation, maintained a high degree of agricultural stability. The history of agriculture in the United States, however, suggests that our farmers would oppose the heavy regulation required to create such stability. Yet whatever stability might be achieved through eliminating government regulations and supports would most assuredly cost us our much-prized system of small to medium-sized family farms.

Since the inception of the New Deal, we have sought to follow a sort of middle path, supporting farmers, albeit imperfectly, in response to changing needs. Some feel that circumstances have now become too complicated, and costs too high, for us to continue on this path. We have arrived at a crossroads in terms of the future of our food production. Whatever our choice, it will profoundly affect how we care for our farmland. If we have any sense that the sacredness of farmland is somehow tied to the image of a small family farm, loss of this system will be a loss in a certain level of consciousness. If and when very large and corporate farms come to dominate food production—which perhaps they already do—our farmland consciousness will be at least mythically impoverished.

In Land Stewardship Project meetings, we sometimes tell a story set in Winona County, in southeastern Minnesota—a lush and rolling green region of dairy farms. That the hilly lands of southeastern Minnesota suffer from erosion can be attested to by the former residents of Beaver. That village, located near the Mississippi River, was literally buried not long ago by repeated mud slides caused by bad farming practices on the surrounding hills. Beaver was a thriving farm community until World War II. Nothing remains of it today.

In 1930, some years before the demise of Beaver, Father Peter Tibesar became the priest of the parish of Holy Trinity in the little town of Rolling Stone, not many miles from where Beaver then stood. A lover of nature, Father Tibesar, with the help of his parishioners, had soon developed a menagerie and a small wildlife refuge. Some local people, it seems, thought of him as a sort of reincarnation of Saint Francis.

Then, in the mid-thirties, Winona County felt the presence of Hugh Bennett's Soil Erosion Service. Two parishioners of Holy Trinity who were cooperators invited "Father Pete" on a tour of their land, and the Father thought, "Yes, this is the way it should be." He began to preach the gospel of land stewardship, and his intensity was such that his parishioners heard him and agreed. Father Tibesar has been dead for many years, but there remains a monument to his life. William Sillman, a retired officer of the SCS, tells us, "Even yet, if I want to show someone an area of pristine conservation practices—terraces, grassed waterways, contoured strips—I take them around to Rolling Stone, show them land which is farmed by the parishioners of Holy Trinity."

This is not, most would agree, a contribution that rivals Hugh Bennett's, but it is a solid and continuing one. And this is a level of influence to which many of us might aspire. In Land Stewardship Project meetings, we suggest that audience members become voices for the land. The right kind of talk, at the grassroots and elsewhere, is deeply important for achieving a turnaround in the way we care for our farmland. If the problem is in large part, as we believe, lack of awareness and commitment, then nothing could be more beneficial to solving it than that each of us, on some level, become an educator.

When we observed with regret the absence of a commitment to a spiritual and ethical vision of our interconnectedness with the land, we were not saying that politics, economics, and technology have no role in the solution. What we are saying is that it is the more fundamental level of our spiritual and ethical vision that determines how we will express ourselves through such disciplines as politics, economics, and technology. Right vision will lead to right action; selfish, narrow vision to wrong.

It has not been fashionable, in recent years, to ask for self-sacrifice and moral commitment as a means of solving social and environmental problems. Instead we have turned to experts and technology, to fossil fuels and finance. This approach has not solved the problem of farmland loss; it seems in fact to have aggravated it, somehow to be at the source of it. We cannot solve problems created by technology with more technology. The answer, we feel, lies elsewhere, and has to do with our increasing commitment to that new-old vision of our interconnectedness with the land.

It may even be that we are now witnessing a momentous shift in human consciousness that will bring us face to face with this vision of interconnectedness. This shift, which perhaps is being pressured into existence by urgent planetary problems, is a change in the basic paradigm or intellectual framework through which we relate to the world. On a very simplistic level, we can describe this as a shift from the machine to the interconnected ecosystem as our primary model for understanding. If we change the framework through which we interrelate with the world, the results of all our actions will likewise change. (The theory of a paradigm shift, as it relates to food production, will be dealt with in a later chapter, "Food Production in the New Paradigm.")

This book will, for the most part, be an exploration of the spiritual and ethical resources that may help us to be good stewards of the land. In the remainder of this section, we will look more closely at the problems in contemporary agriculture and at the implications of being one with—in community with—the land. In section two, we will describe and discuss major religious and cultural visions of how we may relate to the land. In section three, we will consider alternatives to current industrial approaches to food production. If you read through to the epilogue, you will already be involved, and we suggest how you might become *active* in preserving the farmland on this planet, starting in your home community.

To conclude this chapter, here is a Dust Bowl story told by a man named Stanley Schnelle. It can be seen as a parable suggesting the path we must take if we are to find our way through to a successful solution of the problem of farmland loss:

> My God, you could be out, and that wind would start blowing that dust, and it would get dark as it is at night.

> You couldn't walk agin' it at all. Well, I went over to my father-in-law's place. I'd taken the missis over there, and he had a fella working for him by the name of John Lane. And John was goin' out to pull rocks. I says, "John, I'll go out and help you." And we went to load up a bunch of rocks, and the fella says, "Stanley, I believe it's going to rain." I says, "Rain, hell, that's just dust you see a-comin'."
>
> We loaded up the rocks and unloaded them, and went out to where we'd left our pry bar and spade and shovel. And John says, "I don't believe there's any use to loadin' up another load. It's goin' to rain." I says, "That's not rain, that's dust." Well, just about then the storm hit us. And boy, we couldn't see the house! We was maybe a quarter of a mile from the house. We couldn't see where the place was. But them damn horses, they knew where to go, and we started them out. We rode on the stone boat, and we come right to the house, and Marion's father come out, and he says, "What's the matter?" "Nothing," I says, "only it got so black we couldn't see where we was." And you know, it was just so dark, and the fencerows, they was blowed in with dirt and weeds. Anything that dust could catch on, it would stop on that. O, God, they lost a lot of topsoil then.[15]

John and Stanley were blinded by the results of human ignorance and greed, but the complex intuitions and instincts of the draught horses brought them home. The plow horse, of course, has now been shot and fed to mink, transformed into lovely coats and scarves. It is not likely that technology unleashed, "given *its* head," will bring us home, but humanity does have access to that very special "horse sense" displayed by the animals in Stanley's story. When we choose to turn that way—and there are always some who do—the human organism too can sense its way deep into the complex interconnected web of this living universe. Such men and women—be they nature mystics, eco-scientists or farmers—have much to tell us about the wonders of this great living pattern and about the obligations inherent in being a part of it. If we listen to them and act upon what we hear, we will yet find our way home.

NOTES

1. Gerald O. Barney, study director, *The Global 2000 Report to the President* (New York: Penguin Books, 1982), p. 40.
2. Joe Paddock, ed., *The Things We Know Best* (Olivia, MN: Book 200, 1976), p. 102.
3. J. Russell Smith, *Tree Crops* (New York: Devin-Adair, 1950), fig. 1.
4. Lester R. Brown and Edward C. Wolf, *Worldwatch Paper 60: Soil Erosion: Quiet Crisis in the World Economy* (Washington, DC: Worldwatch Institute, 1984), pp. 17–21.
5. Ibid., p. 21.
6. Ibid., pp. 36–39.
7. James Risser, "Iowa Soil Erosion Is Twice U.S. Average," *Des Moines Register*, Nov. 25, 1983, p. 12A.
8. Wendell Berry, *The Unsettling of America* (San Francisco: Sierra Club Books, 1978), p. 11.
9. Linda K. Lee, "Land Use and Soil Loss: A 1982 Update," *Journal of Soil and Water Conservation*, July–August, 1984, p. 228.
10. National Agricultural Lands Study, *The Protection of Farmland: A Reference Guidebook for State and Local Governments* (Washington, DC: U.S. Government Printing Office, 1981), p. 4.
11. Barney, pp. 33–34.
12. T. C. McLuhan, ed., *Touch the Earth* (New York: Pocket Books, 1972), p. 15.
13. Melville H. Cohee in "Out of the Dust Bowl," *Journal of Soil and Water Conservation*, January–February 1984, pp. 8, 9.
14. Wes Jackson, *New Roots for Agriculture* (San Francisco: Friends of the Earth/Land Institute, 1980), p. 55.
15. Paddock, pp. 102–3.

· 2 ·

The Land Organism

Behold this compost! behold it well!
Perhaps every mite has once form'd part of a sick
  person—yet behold!
The grass of spring covers the prairies,
The bean bursts noiselessly through the mould. . .
Out of its little hill faithfully rise the potato's
  dark green leaves,
Out of its hill rises the yellow maize-stalk,
  the lilacs bloom in the dooryards,
The summer growth is innocent and disdainful
  above all those strata of sour dead.

Walt Whitman
from "This Compost"

WE have all now enjoyed—and been made anxious by—a new perspective of planet Earth. From outer space, that which in the atavistic imagination of the human race had always seemed immense, even infinite, now seems small, frail, and vulnerable. From this perspective, what we have always known in our minds becomes more real for us. Observing our beautiful planet Earth from afar, it is clear that its surface is in large part water. Still, it is not so clear from this perspective how little of the remainder, about 11 percent of the total, is rich and productive farmland. An exceptionally large part of this 11 percent exists here in the United States. Such a blessing in land carries with it great hope for our future, and great responsibility.

There are many ways in which we can view land. We can, for instance, look at it as a commodity or an investment, something best described by numbers. It costs X amount and will produce Y amount per acre. It is taxed and its value inflates or deflates at a given numerical rate. We can also look at land with the eyes of those who dream of development, who imagine softball diamonds or tracts of houses where tall corn now rattles in the wind. Or we can narrow our focus and view land through the lens of the soil scientist who tests it for acidity or alkalinity, for its percentage of humus and amounts of certain important minerals.

One of the most fruitful ways of looking at land is as a single complex organism of interrelated parts. Just as a deer or a dog is made up of many interrelated organs (heart, hide, eye, and intestines), land too is made up of interconnected parts or "organs." There is mineral content, of course—in large part eroded or leached from rock. And there is the decayed matter of once living plants and animals. What is often not thought of, however, is the enormous amount of actual life that is present in and part of a healthy soil. We are talking here about insects, worms, nematodes, endless swarms of microorganisms (millions to the teaspoonful), which, in their life processes, break down once living matter into an important constituent of healthy, fertile soil. It has been estimated that an acre of healthy topsoil will contain as much as eleven tons of such soil life. In an interview, Hans Jenny, the dean of American soil scientists, states:

> When I add up the live weights, exclusive of roots, estimated by soil biologists, I find more living biomass below ground than above it, amounting to the equivalent of 12 horses per acre. The soil organisms consume oxygen from the soil air and give off carbon dioxide, and the summation of the multitudes of respirations characterize the metabolism of a soil individual. Hence, I designate soil as a living system.[1]

This living system is a sort of *processing medium* through which old life passes into new. If old life were not constantly broken down into soil, there would soon be no soil and no new life. Within the land organism, we must also include the larger life forms that cyclically rise from it and return to it. We are talking here of plants, animals, and, of course, the human race. Looked at from the point of view we have been describing, all life becomes an extension of land.

Our interconnectedness with the land organism is perhaps most apparent in the food we eat. In recent times, however, awareness of even this connection has weakened. Many children assume that food is somehow produced in the back of supermarkets. They are upset when they learn that hamburger, for instance, was once the fat and muscle of a living animal.

All forms of life, including our own, are "organs" of the greater life cycle. Our bodies, too, must in their time return to the earth, but civilization has in many ways shielded us from the life and death cycles of the land organism. Birth is hidden from the view of most Americans, and death is sanitized in slaughterhouses, hospitals, nursing homes, and funeral parlors. Fertilizer for our fields is drawn from the fluids of plants and animals that lived ages ago and delivered to us in tanks. It is, therefore, hard for us today to really feel in our bones how everything in its time goes back into the earth to feed new life, and yet this may be the most fundamental of all truths. To ignore it is surely a mistake.

For the greater land organism to exist in good health, all life forms, as its organs, must maintain a harmonious balance, or homeostasis. In a healthy system there are no vacant niches waiting to be filled. Any one life form, therefore, can increase only at the expense of others. Should an expansion continue—as in, say, the case of a deer herd when its complementary predatory species are absent—the habitat that sustains this herd becomes overbrowsed. If population growth continues unchecked, habitat damage will in time be so great that the burgeoning population will be cut back in another way, by starvation and disease. A microbe may be substantially smaller than a wolf or a mountain lion, but during conditions of environmental imbalance, it can become far more severe than either in restoring order.

All environmental insights can and must be applied to the human condition. Farmland, for instance, should be seen as primary human habitat, a sine qua non for our existence. It is through farmland that the energy of the universe, of creation, flows into and through us, our lives and our works. This land, however, so important to our well-being, is now rapidly diminishing, both in quantity and quality. Ecological wisdom would have us look hard at and reflect on this developing condition.

When a creature takes from its system without returning, it is a parasite. Should that creature continue to take and expand to the point where it destroys its surrounding environment, it has become a disease. When speaking of the animal inhabitants of the land—our brother and sister creatures here—we unhesitatingly apply such labels. We hesitate, however, when speaking of ourselves. Yet we can increasingly see, in ecological terms, humanity as a planetary disease. We have dug into this earth like a bacteria culture into soft living flesh, and we have spread, gnawing hungrily through link after link of the great chain, leaving our toxic waste everywhere around us.

Our species has been extremely adept at avoiding consequences as our populations have, at the expense of other life forms, enormously expanded. Not that it is wrong for a life form to try to expand to its limits. All living things continually reach for more and more of the light. This is the way of things. But we must accept the fact that there *are* limits. Beyond them lies disaster.

We, unlike the other occupants of this planet, are blessed—and cursed—with foreknowledge. This has allowed us to make saving adjustments within the ecosystem even though our numbers have relentlessly increased. Originally, our consciousness, with its capacity for foreknowledge, was an effective survival tool, but the law of diminishing returns has gone into effect; our environmental manipulations threaten to undercut us. Our consciousness must more and more deal with the results of our own actions.

There is, however, another choice: Because of our capacity for foreknowledge, we could decide to become loving stewards of life. For some this role seems all too troublesome and difficult. To others, at the extreme opposite end of the attitudinal spectrum, it seems arrogant because it assumes we know enough to "guide" nature. But there are others still who believe that, if we are to use ourselves fully, use our full humanness, there is really nothing else we can do. With the results of our carelessness and greed assaulting our eyes at every turn, to do nothing in response is to deny ourselves at a very deep level. Such denial leads to disease, both within ourselves and within the surrounding environment.

From this point of view, for humankind to accept as its role the stewardship of the earth—wherever we find our footprint on it—is for humankind to find its ecological niche. For those of this persuasion, nothing else is nearly as interesting, challenging, or, in the long run, rewarding. And as the imperatives become clearer, more and more of us are in fact getting in step, even if our concern for the environment is in the main limited to those improvements which most quickly enhance our own well-being.

The world of personal desire besieges us everywhere. We do not live in the calm of sacred time, but in a world in which time is a precious and limited commodity. We strap it to our wrists and check with it many times each day. It is easy to see how people who live in such a world would find quality stewardship of land burdensome. We can only suggest that they reconsider their priorities. Human culture has been maturing. We are no longer children of nature. We must give up the privileges of childhood and take on the responsibilities of adulthood. In the example of the good parent, we must be willing to sacrifice for the larger whole.

Those who shun the idea of stewardship because of its human-centered arrogance do, however, offer a valid criticism. If the stewardship concept simply means management of natural resources for short- or medium-term human benefit, one can certainly question whether it is enough. If, however, stewardship implies a desire to serve the long-term well-being of the overall land organism of which we are a part, we then have, not arrogance, but humility before the grandeur of the universe. Such a mature concept of stewardship would require us to be nature-sensitive, recognizing that we live in a world of becoming, always on the cutting edge of creation. Each decision, each action sculpts the world, for good or ill, as it will be.

Condemnation of human arrogance in our relationship to nature should not lead us to denigrate all that is human. We should not deny the goodness in ourselves. The foreknowledge that has led us to try to "bank" the richness of creation can also lead us into true stewardship. Itself an expression of nature, human consciousness should, as it increasingly recognizes the need, contribute to the survival not only of humans, but of the whole of the natural world. To those who regret that we gave up the environmentally benign instincts of other animals in favor of consciousness, one can only answer that for better or worse a hard-won light now burns within us that is one of the glories of creation. Probably our consciousness is only partly kindled. Should we ever know the whole, it is likely that we would no more willingly lay it to waste than chop away our own fingers.

The component parts of the land organism are in dynamic balance. A continual process of adaptation is going on. Each "organ" tries to maintain itself at the point of fullest possible harmony, fullest health. In times of imbalance, of crisis, the land organism experiences sudden rapid changes within its structure; then relative stability returns. We are in a state of imbalance right now, and everywhere on the planet biotic and social adaptation are going on. The writing of this book is an example. So is your reading of it. Or of another with a differing viewpoint. It is important, in this time of upheaval, that we recognize that our way of being on Earth is finally coming home to roost; we, too, are now a threatened species.

NOTES

1. Hans Jenny, "My Friend, the Soil," *Journal of Soil and Water Conservation,* 1984, p. 160.

· 3 ·

What's Wrong with American Agriculture

DESPITE boosterism to the contrary, American agriculture is seething with problems and has been for many years. The overall land organism is experiencing great dis-ease. The soil, the water, and diverse communities of wildlife are suffering, and some members of the farm community have even chosen to take their own lives rather than continue to live within circumstances as they now exist. Others, with increasing frequency, have vented their frustration on members of their families or on their livestock. It is time for us to accept these problems as fact, and to admit that they are not caused solely by a few politicians and corporate decision-makers. Lenders, small businessmen, writers, educators, and many others, including farmers, are also at fault for what has gone wrong.

In recent years it has become common to criticize agricultural industries for their limited vision, along with the politicians and the schools of agriculture which have supported these industries. We have avoided, however, for both good and bad reasons, criticizing the farmer. It is this writer's contention that, if we are to properly maintain our land and our agriculture, we can no longer afford to look the other way. A too-narrow profit motive has dominated farmers as completely as any other group in the system. If this chapter seems to concentrate unduly on the farmer, that is because it seeks to extend arguments already commonly leveled at the rest of the agriculture community. To adapt a sentiment expressed in Edward Abbey's *Monkey Wrench*

Gang, the trouble with the farmer is that he isn't any better than the rest of us. And, as Wes Jackson of the Land Institute has recently been saying in response to our agricultural crisis, we are, in many ways, a fallen people.

A long-term effort to reduce farming to its economic components, while rejecting ecological, sociological, ethical and spiritual aspects, underlies our current difficulties on the land. Narrowly focusing on the economics of agriculture does not, of course, change reality. The latter aspects are as real and important as the economic ones, and by denying the obvious, our agricultural community has brought considerable ruin upon itself. The narrow focus on profit has eliminated checks and balances, and winter winds now blow dark with our diminishing topsoil. Greed has been allowed out of the bag, neighbor has swallowed neighbor, and rural community has begun to die. All too often having a neighbor's land has become more important than having a neighbor. Ironically, reducing agriculture to its economic components has led to a capital intensive approach to farming which, in the absence of a sufficient international market, has brought economic ruin upon a great many American farmers.

Over the past generation or so, agriculture has undergone more change than in all its previous history. During this period, it sold out its original vision or model for a newer and shinier one. The old vision, that of the small family farm, was one of harmony between the farm family and its larger community. Although never given full membership, the land, too, was a part of this community.

The old vision was but a step from being a expression of the eco-model. It had a sense of modesty and balance, and it envisioned farming as a complex, interconnected way of life in which economic values were but a part of the whole. Some farmers harbor a measure of ambivalence about the loss of this vision, but, reluctantly or not, they have, for the most part, let it go.

Adherents to the new vision (or is it blindness?) have criticized this point of view roundly: "Farming," they state, "is not a way of life, but a business." To believe otherwise is to be a sentimental fool.

This new linear approach rejected sociology and ecology (and all the rest) and called the farmer a businessman, the farm a factory. Somewhere in the 1960s or early seventies, this vision became dominant in the mind of the American agricultural community, and in a 1985 speech former Secretary of Agriculture Orville Freeman called American agriculture "the greatest production plant in the world."[1] The beginnings of this shift, of course, had occurred much earlier: when the farmer abandoned the horse and manure in favor of the tractor and chemicals, soon becoming our major consumer of industrial goods, it was well on its way. As mentioned earlier, this new capital intensive, consumptive tendency is the limb upon which many farmers have recently been left hanging.

Our land grant schools of agriculture have been trailblazers in this shift to the corporate approach. Seldom do they teach a course in sociology, ecology, or ethics. Such subjects have been "externalized" from the curriculum. "Ag" professors briskly wave the flag of high tech instead. A dean of the University of Minnesota School of Agriculture has, in fact, been quoted as saying, "The misconception is that agriculture means farming."[2] And the agricultural future envisioned and advanced by most of these schools is clearly *not* farming.

The shift in identity from farmer to businessman has gone further, I believe, than even most farmers have yet recognized. For many years the specter of corporate agriculture dominating American farmland has been held above our heads. I would argue, however, that the long awaited—and feared—creature is already among us. Somewhere in the past twenty years, farmers, if you will, became the tail end of the assembly line.

Most, perhaps, felt there was little choice. Through education, lending pressure, peer pressure, the extension service, advertising, and a host of other forces, farmers were inexorably levered into this system. The free ham dinners with cocktails, which agribusiness was beginning to offer farm groups, put them but one step below the three-martini lunch league. Many farmers found such consideration deeply seductive. Once they had moved into this system, though still believing themselves among the most independent of human beings, they in fact found little freedom of choice. With visions of greatly increased prosperity dancing before their eyes, it was the rare individual who seriously resisted.

It seemed strange at first to hear the new language of farmers, the "bottom-line" language of business. Somewhere in the 1970s any farmer "who amounted to anything" was no longer a farmer but an "owner-operator." Not only did he take on a new language, he also gave up his person as advertising space: his cap, jacket, and shirt now speak the hard, linear language of chemistry, technology and inbred seeds. Forty years ago the straw hat was exchanged for a John Deere or Allis Chalmers cap. Our current generation of farmers sports labels like ConAgra, Impro, Banvel, and Lorsban. As a symbolic statement, working daily on our thoughts and actions, this offering of the body as advertising space is no small matter.

As long as the seemingly endless spiral of land inflation continued, there was little complaining, save from those who wanted to get in on it. In concert with the overall agricultural establishment, the farm community rejected ecological values and embraced growth and the idea of the farm as factory. Those who were cautious, who tended to hold to the old model, were confused, even a little ashamed of their self-restrained farming operations. Their more "courageous" neighbors were emerging as paper millionaires. For many of these aggressive owner-operators growth had become "a way of life." One million wasn't enough, and they borrowed against this paper (fatal flaw) in the pursuit of more millions.

There was, of course, increasing craziness in their lives. Sincere food producers, for example, had to compete with those who invested in farming for a tax loss. But this financial game-playing proved fascinating to many farmers and began to influence the way they handled their own finances. This kind of "distortion" now permeates much of what was originally useful and good-intentioned in American agriculture. Many argue that at this time agriculture's original primary purpose—the growing of healthy food—was subordinated to and got lost among its economic components.

The fencerow-to-fencerow production called for in the early seventies by Secretary of Agriculture Earl Butz was, for all practical purposes, posited on an infinite market. Mr. Butz had misread the future. The world market for U.S. agricultural commodities has recently proven to be limited, and overproduction has glutted it, causing farm prices to fall below the cost of that production. For a time farmers survived by borrowing against the ever-growing value of their land, but with the collapse in 1981 of a forty-year inflationary spiral of land values, it has all, of course, crumbled. Notes have been called in. "Millionaires" have been foreclosed on. Ownership of land is shifting a little deeper into the system, toward the corporate level.

At least for the moment, those farmers who own their land and had cautiously held their ground tend to be surviving, and farm groups like the Amish that have retained their self-sufficient ecological approaches have remained relatively unscathed. Elsewhere folks are shaking their heads sadly over the new misery on the land, but they observe that farming is, after all, a business like any other. Where is that lender today who will say, as was so common in the thirties, "Stay where you are; pay me when you can"?

On a recent protest trip to Washington, D.C., a farmer I know found himself on an elevator with a Midwest senator who is also a famous businessman. In response to my friend's complaints, the senator offered him a tip: "Sell out now, and when land bottoms out, buy back in again and ride the next inflationary spiral. You'll make a killing."

There is, of course, no way to sell out in today's land market that would allow a farmer to buy back in at a future time. But there is more than this to criticize in the senator's response. Home, life-style, neighborhood, complexities of food production and of caring for livestock, the specific knowledge of a piece of land—these were disregarded in that advice, erased as easily as numbers in an investment portfolio.

For those, however, who bought into the new model of agriculture, there can be very little legitimate complaining. Farming, they have insisted, is not a life-style, but a business. We must be very careful what we sow, for that we will surely reap.

Despite the senator's limited focus, it has often seemed that most legislators have wanted to be helpful, to give our farmers what they need, or, to be more accurate, want. Their eyes turn misty when the *old image* of the farmer is called to mind: Jefferson's yeoman landholder, the foundation of our democracy, living on and working the land with his family, surviving against odds and the weather and feeding the rest of us at bargain rates. For a couple of generations now we have all wanted to help this fellow to hold on and continue with his essential work.

The powers that be in agriculture have known how to exploit this desire. They have known as well how to exploit the ignorance of farm economics within our legislatures. The agricultural lobby, now dominated, not by farmers, but by a hodgepodge of commodity groups and agribusiness associations, has been a slippery devil, a magician that manages to pull off the same set of tricks each time a new farm bill is written. Tax breaks and price supports are introduced to save the struggling, beginning or otherwise marginal farmer. Support, however, is then almost always extended to *all* farmers, no matter how large or wealthy. Then comes the kicker: the various forms of aid are doled out according to the dollar-amount of a farmer's purchase or on a per-unit-of-production basis. Therefore, the more a farmer produces, the larger his purchases, the more taxpayer support he gets. The lion's share of aid has always gone into the pockets of those who produce and spend the most. By and large this means those who are wealthiest. Under the Reagan administration, 60 percent of government farm aid has gone to the largest 17 percent of U.S. farms.[3]

The final destination of most government farm aid has not, however, been the farmer at all. Our new agriculture has been designed to be as capital intensive as possible, and a very large percentage of taxpayer support (and farm earnings) is, therefore, quickly channeled into the coffers of the manufacturers and sellers of agricultural chemicals and machinery. To again quote Wes Jackson, "Our farmers merely launder money for 'ag' industries." Farmers themselves, in their new language, have been saying, "My cash flow is great, but I can't get any of it to stop." And most of the value of the inflated land prices of the seventies, we should note, was siphoned off by the agribusiness complex, leaving farmers, even many who were once millionaires, shaking an empty tank.

Providing public aid to farmers according to their volume of production has, of course, falsely stimulated production, putting unnecessary strain on the land. It has also resulted in increased, but ultimately unnecessary, purchases from (and profits for) agricultural suppliers. Tax incentives which increase with the size of a purchase also enhance sales and therefore profits for support businesses.

Because there is profit to be made through falsely stimulating production, more economical and ecologically sound alternatives are almost always rejected. When, for example, the suggestion is made that we solve the problem of weak markets by cooperatively limiting production (thereby taking the strain off expensive-to-farm marginal lands), powerful interest groups within the agricultural lobby have always managed to steer things back to taxpayer support of overproduction. This overblown situation could not last forever, and as farmers have lost their equity, businesses immediately dependent on them have also begun to fail.

One wonders if our legislators have clearly understood the effects of their decisions. Surely some of them must have. The continuing losers have been, of course, the land, the taxpayers, and those struggling farmers in whose name all of this has gone on—50,000 of whom are expected to go out of business in 1986.[4]

An ironic aspect of this system is that the marginal farmer has so often supported it, and not, for the most part—one almost wishes it were—out of ignorance. For one thing, most of these farmers believe in independent competitiveness. Down deep they tend to feel the victor deserves his spoils. After talking with a great many such farmers, I am persuaded that, at least until very recently, all too many of them have been hoping and believing that they too would in time become "big" and therefore able to benefit from this system. We have expected it at other levels of our society, but who would ever have thought that the economic mythos of F. Scott Fitzgerald would in time become so appropriate to the American farmer: tomorrow he will run faster, stretch out his arms farther, and one fine day . . .

Conservation and its demands complicate matters for anyone who would deal with agriculture as a purely economic system. The powers that be have, for instance, resisted for years the idea of cross-compliance, the tying of government benefits to care of the land. The occasional set-aside, such as Payment-in-Kind in 1983—which could so easily have become a useful conservation tool (and PIK was originally sold as such)—has in the long run been written or administered so as to avoid serious conservation demands.

In fact, when it comes to establishing a set-aside land base for which a farmer will receive payments, those who have had their marginal land in soil-preserving crops have always been penalized. That is, since this marginal land is already out of cash crop production, they receive no benefits for retiring it. And with the continuing exception of a small but tough core of conservationists, farmers have gone along with this approach, even pushed for it. Finally, it is not the mainstream of agriculture that we have to thank for positive conservation legislation written into the 1985 Farm Bill, but a broad coalition of environmental, church, and progressive farm organizations.

Too many farmers seem to have loved, not so much their land, as their ownership of that land. They balk at the idea that owning land is a privilege which carries with it basic responsibilities. Private and governmental organizations that seek to put limits on "what owners can do with their own land" are almost universally feared and hated. For years, for example, on the northern prairies of the United States, a bitter fight has been ranging between farmers and departments of natural resources over the preservation of remaining prairie potholes. When soybean prices were very high a few years back, some Midwest farmers actually plowed and planted their lawns. In one county in central Minnesota that was already more than 90 percent under the plow, a hiking trail along an abandoned railroad right-of-way was bitterly opposed for fear that this narrow corridor would become a breeding ground for "noxious weeds."

In recent years, when talk turned to "sodbuster" legislation, legislation that would withdraw government benefits from farmers for opening up highly erodible marginal lands, most agreed that a retroactive approach would be essential to keep many farmers from immediately plowing their pastures and bulldozing their woodlots to make that land safe for future production. Finally, as was made clear in chapter one, most farmers, tacitly supported by the rest of the agricultural establishment, have resisted becoming involved in a serious conservation program. One Nebraska farmer, when questioned about loss of topsoil on his land, answered, "It's dirt all the way down." The Soil Conservation Service is tolerated and minimally funded within the U.S. Department of Agriculture just so long as no one is forced to use its services. All of this tends to support Wendell Berry's insight that the problems of rural America may not be so much problems of economics as of character. Not, of course, that this deficiency begins as we leave the city limits.

It has pained me to write the above two paragraphs. I know many, many farmers who have deeply loved and devotedly cared for their land, but they are far from the majority, and it is very important, at this time, that we do not pretend otherwise.

It is unacceptable that we continue, in such large part, to abandon the management of U.S. farmland, the most important farmland base in the world, to the chaotic impulses of individual and corporate greed. We must not let the bottom line dominate our decisions about this resource base, for in truth, as the district conservationist of the region where I live recently told me, the bottom line has nothing to do with money gained or lost, but with the amount of soil washed to the bottom of the hill.

Any sane farm program must take into account the well-being of the land and limit production to expected demand. These two aims are, of course, fully interconnected. Overproduction caused by confusion, unwillingness to cooperate, poor policy-making, and greed has been the single most destructive economic factor in the life of American agriculture. Victor Ray, formerly a vice president of the National Farmers Union and the board chairman of the Land Stewardship Project, recently wrote that "the singular cause of the problems of agriculture is overproduction. It is bankrupting farmers. It is causing a devastating depletion of topsoil and underground water. It is endangering the entire economy. Partisans in the fight for a farm bill," he continues, "should not be diverted by such details as loan levels, target prices, payment for set asides, etc. The key feature is how much it will reduce production."

Ray believes that a conservation reserve of at least 50 million, perhaps even 100 million acres is necessary to raise prices significantly enough for us to begin to solve our agricultural problems. "We cannot," he states, "save the rural economy, and we cannot save the soil and water resources unless we cut production, and not just a little, but a lot."[5]

The majority of farmers, however, their eyes fixed on a distant glimmer, have been unwilling or unable to cooperatively limit production—or even to cooperatively set prices, as the National Farmers Organization has been attempting to get them to do for many years. As we shall see in chapter seven, the key rural American myths—the competitive frontier and Horatio Alger myths—have motivated us, not to hang together at modest levels, but to attempt to rise individually to the top of the ladder. American farmers, unlike, say, their European cousins, have been unwilling to accept limitations on a power they feel in their bones. They know that there are hungry people in the world, that there is a market out there somewhere. What they want is elbow room and the green light to produce for this market. They want all-out production. At a fair profit.

Unfortunately, producing food for the world, as we have recently found, is a very complicated matter. Our willingness to use food as a weapon in the form of embargoes has cost us something of the world market. Despite our enormous production and farm incomes that are often below the cost of that production, our capital intensive methods and the international strength of the dollar have tended to make us less than competitive with several other food-producing nations. And those who most need our food often cannot afford to pay for it. Nor should we, on moral grounds, encourage a system that makes poor nations dependent on us for food when there is any possibility of their producing their own.

It may well be that agriculture will remain the greatest hope in our efforts to deal with a bad international balance of trade. However, the thought of balancing America's soil against America's appetite for the planet's resources makes one cringe. To assume, then, that the way to solve the crisis in American agriculture is all-out production for the world market is, one must believe, immature, heavy-handed, and born of greed and bad thinking. This approach will enable us merely to stay aboard a sinking ship, laying on patches for dear life. At least one heartland state has even considered a lottery to help keep farmers afloat. Far better that we face reality, that we consider the plan to cut production through land set-asides, even though it will demand a discipline and humility not previously seen in our agricultural decision making.

It is too late to hope—even if we were to accept Victor Ray's sensible set-aside suggestion—that we might get out of our present crisis without further misery. His plan does, however, put our feet onto the hard ground we must walk. Taxpayer support would be needed during the period of transition, but it would be less expensive than our current system of supports. The 1985 Farm Bill is expected to cost taxpayers $52 billion over the next three years, and no one expects it to solve anything. A sum like that would go a long way toward switching agriculture onto a new and far healthier track.

Almost everyone agrees that the structure of American agriculture will soon be quite changed. Mainstream thinking has it that all significant food production will come from either extremely large individually owned farms or from corporate entities that will now not only control farmers but own land. At least one estimate suggests that as few as 100,000 farms will dominate American agriculture. This would seem to be the logical conclusion of a process that began a long time ago. Within this system, high tech will prevail, and we are unlikely to mistake such agriculture for farming.

There are, of course, other possible agendas. Section three of this book, "Whole Vision," describes a number of them. These are alternative, ecological approaches to food production which in part at least are based on a return to the vision of the family farm. From one perspective, the choice is between people on the land and technology on the land. That is, we could, to some degree, withdraw from capital intensive farming. One farmer at the tail end of the agricultural assembly line can easily manage a thousand acres of flat prairie land. Or two or three thousand. But once he has invested in machines, there is no place for the full-time hired hand or even sons and daughters; both the money and the need that would have kept them there are gone. We must admit that, at least until the world's petroleum runs out, it would be possible for 1 percent or less of our population to produce our food. If that is what we want.

It is not that people can't raise food as well as machines and chemicals can. In describing the production "miracle" wrought by our technology, we seldom mention that we hold most of the best land in the best growing climates in the world. Furthermore, we focus on man-hour efficiency. One farmer feeds seventy-six nonfarmers—or whatever the current number. (The factory workers who support the farmer are, of course, never included as farm workers.) Perhaps a more accurate approach would be to compare the amount of food grown *per acre* around the world. From this perspective, we are far from the most productive nation.

If, for instance, we were to "garden" our farmland—as the Chinese do much of theirs, with 80 percent of their huge population growing food—we could raise far more on a per acre basis than we now do. Instead, we have freed most of our people to produce beer can holders, power toothbrushes, and the latest version of the hula hoop. Or freed them from employment altogether. By investing in farmers rather than machines, we could employ far more people to raise our food on far less land. And the land then used would be that which is most suitable for agriculture. The rest could be allowed to heal itself and, in certain ways, us.

We must finally, however, ask if American farmers truly do want to continue farming within a modest, steady-state system. Obviously none of them want to lose their life's work to a lender, but a lot of the enthusiasm for the new approach to farming had to do with a desire to be liberated from the old. And the desire to move to town, away from the isolation and hard work of the farming way of life, has been a continuing and powerful thread in rural history. Anyone who has grown up in the country knows how "hungry" many farm people, especially wives and children, have been to get to town. Unlike most of our European forebears and the Native Americans who preceded us on this land, the farming community has always lived spread out, each family in its own, often lonely, domain.

In some ways, given the great growth in farm size, the sense of isolation today is as intense as it ever was, even with television and improved transportation. It is even hard for young farmers to find wives willing to live in rural isolation. Many farmers who sold out high in the seventies are now happy to be living in the embrace of small rural towns. They do not want to buy back in. Many still on the farm were simply holding out for a better deal and got caught when the deflation in land values began in 1981. In short, despite much popular sentiment to the contrary, farming as previously experienced in America may not be the best of all possible life-styles. If and when larger populations return to the land, human issues will demand at least as much energy and creativity as economic ones.

It seems to this writer that the Faustian myth might help us to understand what has gone wrong on the American land. Faust sold his soul to the devil for wealth and power, luxury and ease. What did we give up when we embraced the economic and technological vision and turned our backs on the overall health of the land organism and its communities? And what did we get in the bargain? Flights to Honolulu, to Las Vegas, to the Holy Land. The devil, not lacking in business acumen, had a contract with Faust. The good times were not to last forever; in four-and-twenty years he was to return for his due.

Recently, in a tiny country church ten miles from my home in central Minnesota, I listened to C. Dean Freudenberger discuss many of the issues contained in this chapter. He has written books and has traveled the globe for many years in an effort to help move humankind toward saner ways of producing food and caring for farmland. He clearly does not care for the capital intensive methods of contemporary farming. I asked him why then he called for a moratorium on foreclosures on such farms (I was seeking an explanation beyond his obvious sympathy for human suffering). His answer, if I understood him right, was that we must, if at all possible, keep our farmers in place *with their memories*—not only their good memories of the land and its needs, but also *their memories of what has gone wrong,* so that we will not so easily make the same mistakes again.

NOTES

1. Orville Freeman, speech at "Food, Farming and the Future" Symposium, Concordia College, Moorhead, MN, September, 1985.
2. Jim Dawson, "Farm Crisis Felt at College of Agriculture," *Minneapolis Star and Tribune,* Nov. 4, 1985, p. 13A.
3. Jim Hightower, "The Reagan Administration's Cynical Response to the Farm Crisis," *Utne Reader,* December 1984/January 1985, p. 89.
4. CBS Television news report, Monday, Feb. 24, 1986.
5. Victor Ray, in "1985 Farm Bill: Another Chance for the Soil," *The Land Stewardship Letter,* Summer 1985, p. 5.

·4·

The Reluctant Evolution of a Land Ethic

IN *A Sand County Almanac*, published in 1949, Aldo Leopold established the basic premises for a land ethic. He also stated that nothing as important as an ethic is ever written. He was, of course, right. An ethic must evolve within the collective consciousness of a people in accordance with environmental realities. Our evolution toward a land ethic since Leopold's book has been extremely slow. One might assume, then, that a land ethic is very complex and difficult to understand. Such, however, is not the case. A land ethic is really no more complicated than the Golden Rule. The stumbling block continues to be, as it was forty years ago, when Leopold wrote, that we are unwilling to extend this rule to include the nonhuman—the land.

We have been unable to take that step because to do so would be to undermine the worldview upon which Western civilization has been built. To accept the idea that the land is not just a resource for humans, that it has rights and we are bound by responsibilities to it, will dramatically change our way of being here. Nothing less than the great planetary dis-ease of our times could compel us to make such a change, but make it we must, it appears, if we are to survive.

In the late nineteenth century, the Nez Percé Indian Smohalla expressed his disapproval of the white man's pragmatic attitude toward the land:

> "You ask me to plow the ground. Shall I take a knife and tear my mother's breast? Then when I die she will not take me to her bosom to rest.
>
> "You ask me to dig for stone. Shall I dig under her skin for her bones? Then when I die I cannot enter her body to be born again.
>
> "You ask me to cut grass and make hay and sell it and be rich like the white men. But how dare I cut off my mother's hair?"[1]

The Native American worldview could hardly be more unlike the one upon which Western civilization has been built. Ours has been anthropocentric, human-centered. In it, we are separate from the land, and the land exists to provide us with the raw materials necessary for life and a continuously expanding materialistic civilization. For Smohalla, the land was at least as alive and sacred as he was, and therefore he had to show great restraint in his use of it. It is clear that his view and the ethic it implies would not have allowed Western civilization out of the starting blocks. It is clear, too, that we in the developed nations would have to give up a great deal of what we now take for granted if we were to abide by it.

Were it not for rapidly mounting and painful evidence that Smohalla's worldview is brimming with truth, it is unlikely that we would or could ever make the basic shift that would bring the land within our ethical system. But in light of all we now know, how can anyone refute what poets, mystics, and "primitives" have known intuitively since the emergence of human consciousness: the natural world is a living system with which we are fully and deeply interconnected. The old dualistic approach will not stand up; we are one with nature. When we injure it, we ultimately injure ourselves. Though we may never become as respectful of the land as Smohalla chose to be, we must begin, and very soon, to accept his basic premises.

Having entered an enormously rich, virgin continent, our nonnative ancestors were able for generations to ignore the need for a land ethic. Land was so abundant that, even in the early twentieth century, there were those who bragged they had worn out three or four farms in a lifetime. They neither felt guilt nor experienced disapproval from their peers. After the Dust Bowl of the 1930s, it seemed as if we had learned the lesson, but ingenuity and industry found an enormously profitable way to postpone the inevitable. Agriculture began to import petroleum-based fertility to the land. We dug a little deeper into the stored wealth (and health) of our planet. But with our capacity to destroy land exponentially increased by twentieth century technology, we are now, once again, reaching our limits, and the healing potential of a land ethic again beckons.

It was the abundance of land in America that allowed our grandparents to ignore the need for a land ethic. Beyond this, the health of the land, its capacity to fight back, led to an adversarial relationship. Farmers do not live so simply and flexibly on the land as did the Native Americans who preceded them, and as they turned the grass upside down, a battle began that has raged ever since.

In its efforts to heal itself, to return to its former wholeness, the land organism fought back. Farmers' crops were threatened with "weeds," insects, and great migratory flights. The farmer countered with the technology and chemical weapons that have since tipped the balance in his favor. But the sense of being in competition with the land, even though the contest has become one-sided, still lingers. Only grudgingly does the farm community acknowledge that we must relent in our efforts to dominate the land.

A dialogue between the values of competition and cooperation must underlie any serious discussion of an ethic. In America the frontier experience coupled with our free enterprise approach to business has led us to value competition more than cooperation. Our great-grandparents as pioneers did struggle with a hostile environment, but they were also fed, housed, and otherwise cared for through the "generosity" of that environment. And if we are over 35 or so, we can remember a time when cooperation in neighborhoods and communities was much stronger than it is now. This cooperation, essential to the lives of our pioneer forebears, is something we often forget when we discuss our American heritage.

In a different context, in a book called *Inner Tennis*, W. Timothy Gallway, a tennis professional, expresses a theory that links competition and cooperation. Our culture tends to put so much emphasis on beating our opponents that some people have developed a distaste for competitive games. Gallway, though having sympathy for this point of view, feels that he is morally bound to play his best against his opponents. In so doing, he will force them to their best efforts, thereby helping them to perfect their human potential. Competition risen to this moral level transcends itself and becomes, in fact, a form of cooperation.[2] It is such competition that hones ecosystems to their finest pitch of health. Each population culls and combs many others. It is only when competitors seek to *destroy* their opponents, when they lose sight of the fact that we are ultimately in the service of something greater than ourselves—that competition becomes a bad thing.

Leopold wrote that any ethic is based on the recognition that we live in a community of interdependent parts. By its nature, a community is an expression of cooperation, but one aspect of that cooperation is respect for the legitimate growth needs of the individuals within it. The well-being of each is necessary to that of the whole. Every individual or part of the community is to some extent dependent on every other. Yet these exchanges must not seriously damage any single part. An ethic expresses the rules of this sense of being in community with others.

Choices dictated by these rules are usually quite clear-cut. A South Dakota farmer I know, for instance, has had no trouble getting those who hunt his land to help in the maintenance of his wildlife-producing windbreaks. The logic is clear. If we tend to say we are not in community with the land, but in fact we are, that denial will in time lead to the diminishment of the overall community, including ourselves. As we know, in many parts of the world, at many times in history, human denial of the health rights of land has diminished the life of human populations. The checks and balances created through a shared ethic tend to work as an early warning system for the much harsher ones the natural world will surely impose if we are not generous in our ethical relationships.

With those who continue to deny that we are truly in community with land, we can still argue for an ethic of care by asserting that we are part of the ongoing stream of humanity, and therefore responsible to the needs of the human future. This has been the approach of those who see farmland conservation as *resource management.* Their characteristic admonition is that we must pass along land to our grandchildren in as good shape as when we began our use of it. One landowner recently responded to this contention with a question, "What have my grandchildren ever done for me?"

Such a response may sound heartless, but, if we look at what, in fact, we are leaving our grandchildren, it more accurately reflects our true attitude than most of us would like to admit. It cannot be denied, however, that we are in historical continuum with all of humanity—past, present, and future—and the proper question is not "What have our grand*children* ever done for us?" but "What did our grand*parents* do for us?" Our problems are different from those of our grandparents, but their suffering was at least equal to our own, and we do owe something to the future. How we deal with our current land problems will surely bear upon those who follow us here.

To the degree that we ignore our historical (and ethical) connectedness with the stream of human life, we are impoverished. In such isolation, our lives lack large meanings. We are little more than a vague spread of appetities. This, of course, describes the modern alienation upon which so many have commented.

Leopold wrote that approval and disapproval within the community is the basic control mechanism for an ethic. Our deep sensitivity to the opinions of those around us makes it clear how interconnected we are. One might argue that binding law and awareness of and love for "the other" also govern our ethical behavior, but it is clear that, when in community with others, we are in a continual process of adaptation to their opinions. Almost no one is willing to be considered bad or evil, and it can, in fact, be argued that we do not express serious antisocial (perhaps even antiecological) tendencies until such forces as acceptance, respect, and love, which bind us to the overall community, have been denied us.

For many rural landholders, the frontier experience lingers in a philosophy of rugged individualism. Their peer group, presumably small, tends to favor a competitive relationship to the land. In that such a group is unlikely to criticize its members for harsh use of their land, the control mechanism Leopold described as necessary to the functioning of a land ethic is nonexistent. However valuable rugged individualism may have proven in pioneer circumstances, once the map has been filled, such an approach becomes increasingly counterproductive. (In fact, as the biosphere becomes increasingly crowded, the sociological and ecological "value" of an individual may well be judged by the width of community with which he or she ethically identifies.) The ruggedly individualistic landholder can easily develop a dualism that rejects correction from the external world. It is from such a psychic region that rise the words, "It's my land, and I'll do what I want with it."

Landholders, of course, have the most to fear from widespread adoption of a land ethic. The rest of us should, therefore, avoid doing anything that will unnecessarily foster divisiveness. The land organism, as our model, reminds us that we are in community with those whose work puts food on our tables. With sympathy, political support, and a willingness to accept personal sacrifice (some of which will be financial), we should make clear to landholders that they are in community with the rest of society. They must know that if they make the sacrifices necessary for maintaining the long-term health of their land, they will receive the support of the rest of us.

Despite this need to maintain a cohesive relationship with landholders, the overall community must, nevertheless, insist on high standards for the care of farmland. From the larger perspective, the land "belongs" to itself (or, if you prefer, to God), which is another way of saying that it "belongs" to all of us. By our silence, by our reluctance to consider the needs of the land, we all become accomplices in its destruction. Each citizen of the land community has the right and the responsibility to see that the land is not abused. The rural tendency to mind one's own business when someone is abusing the land must be reversed. As Milo Hanson, a farmer who has often stood alone in declaring the rights of land once told me, the sharks in the Gulf of Mexico have no need for our topsoil.

There are those among us whose decisions and actions have a much greater effect on the health of the land organism than do those of the individual farmer. These are the policy makers, the writers, educators, lenders, "ag" officials, and corporate leaders whose decisions affect what thousands of people will do on and with the land for long periods of time. Many corporate land management firms, for example, following the designs of educator-visionaries, require in their operations no conservation measures at all. Such organizations frequently earn a percentage of the *gross* income of the farms they manage rather than of actual profits. They therefore encourage, for themselves, big cash-flow, chemical-intensive farming methods, which are by no means the kindest to the land.

Other profit-oriented visionaries are now working to extend the gasohol market, thereby adding the insatiable American appetite for energy to the already excessive demands on our farmland. That the common source of gasohol is corn, an erosion-producing row crop, makes this approach to energy conservation especially unacceptable. And yet farmers and government officials have worked hand in glove with business in support of these and many other land-damaging schemes. Those who promote policies with such enormous potential for harm to the land should be met with a full chorus of disapproval from the overall community. On the other hand, we should go out of the way to reward those who do the good work of restoring and preserving the land.

Most who resist community acceptance of a land ethic do so on practical grounds. They even argue that those who favor a binding land ethic are being irresponsible. This, as I see it, is psychological projection. Freud told us that we must look for a thing in its opposite. The practical, looked at over a long enough period of time, finds an identity with the ethical. In fact, for an absolute utilitarian, the ethical might be defined as long-term, wide-ranging practicality. The assertion that we have to ease up on soil conservation if we expect to feed the world, when looked at from the long-term perspective, is absurd. It might be possible to justify a plow-out of easily erodible pasture land in terms of immediate personal need, but certainly not in terms of responsible long-range practicality.

Those who are embarrassed by the idea of acting from other than practical premises—and there are many such around—might find it enlightening to consider how the results of our actions return to us. These returns are often subtle, but they are relevant and, I believe, unfailing. In recent years, for example, when agriculture began increasingly to focus on economics, at the expense of neighborhood and community, slowly but surely neighborhood and community began to wane and farms began to manifest themselves as production factories or economic units. These farms no longer express life and beauty, only a certain kind of efficiency. At particular times of the year, their fields may even be dangerous to walk upon. They are a return on the narrow techno-economic focus of contemporary agriculture.

Religion wrote the book on understanding how our actions are returned to us: "Cast your bread upon the waters" and "As ye sow, so shall ye reap." These biblical statements are so familiar that we tend to forget the deep truth they contain. And everywhere around us we see those who seem to have "gotten by," even been rewarded for selfish action. The farmer who invested in chemical fertilizer rather than conservation may seem to have a larger "account with the world" than his less selfish neighbor, but if we take enough such rope, we hang ourselves. In the case of our current "ag" crisis, the selfish action of the individual has boomeranged on the collective level.

Oriental religions have focused very specifically on this idea of a return on thoughts and actions. Termed *karma* in Buddhism and Hinduism, this understanding of how the world sooner or later pays us "in kind" for our actions is deep and highly refined. Karma is looked at, not so much as a moral response to our actions, as an operation of natural law. Selfish, short-term choices, then, are really a product of poor judgment. In time, we surely have to pay for them. If religious insight is valid, it would seem that ethical behavior is very practical indeed.

We must ask, then, what ideas and actions make up the ethical approach to farmland that will produce good feedback, good karma for us in coming generations. In the abstract, the answers seem relatively simple. Our first ethical premise should be that we limit our use of the land to what is essential. This choice is, of course, at odds with American society, which works around the clock to maximize production and consumption of material goods. At almost every turn of the head (or dial) we receive a message, cunningly tied to our most basic desires, to buy and consume.

This continuing barrage will make it very difficult for us to change our habits. Still, if we do not want to pay the penalties of the law of karma, we must stop "gorging ourselves" with what is even more basic than the seed grain—that is, the land itself. If we are to be ethical citizens within the stream of humanity and the overall land organism, we must decide what we need from the land to remain well fed and healthy and try to limit ourselves to this.

Rather than maximum consumption, then, we should choose a level of voluntary simplicity. Such material simplicity is not something to fear; indeed, every wise man who ever lived has been its advocate. Until we disencumber ourselves from excessive desire, excessive accumulation, we cannot begin to live authentically. Once having done so, we are free to leave the kindergarten of human affairs and begin to explore the potential of our lives.

A second ethical premise for our relationship with farmland is that we must find methods that are in harmony with the land organism. These, if possible, will flow with its forces rather than dominating or eliminating them. We are talking here, of course, about various local and solar approaches to energy production and biological approaches to farming. Since these greatly limit industrial inputs, modern agriculture has made every effort to guide us away from them.

The first generation of industrial technology seemed a great boon to those who worked the land:

> If you had a bunch of cattle, the kids had to pump and pump, pumping so much that we was *so* sick and tired of it. For all the livestock and all the horses and pigs, cows and chickens and everything. That took an awful lot of water. And then Daddy got us a gasoline engine. Boy, was that ever something. That was the best thing that Daddy could have ever got us. Then we didn't have to pester ourself pumping any more. The engine was doing it for us. That was nice.[3]

Though one wonders where the windmill was, the first gasoline pump, for its moment, made a heaven of the lives of kids who had hand-pumped water for livestock. And it did little harm to their environment. But our grandfathers loved those machines overly much, were so fascinated with them that the machines soon became their own end, and the generations of technology that followed added less and less to the quality of the lives of those who employed them. In fact, these advances increasingly destroyed the life-style they were meant to ease. On our farmland, as elsewhere, technology has run away with us.

A third premise for an ethical relationship to farmland is that we work to build back—or allow to heal back—the portion of our farmland that we have damaged. This is the work of a mature people, risen to some degree of selflessness. It will require patience, understanding, and humility, but even as we struggle with such work, we deepen in knowledge and character. Commitment to this healing work is at the heart of a healthy coevolution of humanity with the land.

A purely practical approach to ethics may seem enormously deficient. Such a narrowing of focus may in fact be our problem. It takes into account too little of the human spectrum. The reductive economic and factory models for life create, finally, boredom, and many who work in social and ecological movements have begun to recognize an ethical hunger in people. In time we long for righteous behavior, behavior that is psychically and spiritually uplifting. The cynic will mock this—the cynic in each of us—but, when we live righteously, we live in a different dimension. We are no longer alienated from the rest of creation. When we think and act, live for the whole, pettiness falls away and we experience wholeness. Comparatively speaking, we live in a state of grace.

I recall that somewhere in Joseph Conrad's work—I have never been able to find it again—he wrote that he believed that very few things are truly important for us to know, *and all of us know them.* The ethical sense, surely, must be among these things. "Do unto others as you would have them do unto you." In relation to other human beings, at least, we know the rightness of this in our bones. Most of us had a grasp of it even as children. In relation to the land, its karmic corollary is that, in time, the land will do unto us as we have done unto it.

An ethic is not a list of rules to be memorized; it is something deeper and simpler. But this is not to diminish the value of the three ethical premises just noted:

1. We should take no more from the land than is necessary. (This implies acceptance of an appropriate level of voluntary simplicity.)
2. We should develop land-use technologies that flow with the forces of the land rather than against them. (The nine precepts of biological design developed by the advocates of New Alchemy, which have been listed in section three of this book, will lead to better understanding of this premise.)
3. We must work to (or allow to) heal back that portion of the land we have damaged.

The following suggestions will also help us to allow the realization of our larger self and the land ethic it implies:

- We should affirm the idea that the land is far more than a human resource.
- We should be on guard against those who would limit our conception of land to its economic values.
- We who do not own land should nevertheless assume an appropriate level of responsibility for care of the land.
- We should resist the tendency to feel in competition or at war with the land.
- We should acknowledge that there is a limit to how much abuse the land can absorb and still remain healthy. Any use of it should be tied to the concept of long-term sustainability.
- We should try to imagine what the long-range returns will be on any decision or action which affects the land.
- We should continually work to develop our awareness of the land as a living community of interdependent parts that includes us, and we should strive to interpret all phenomena in terms of this web of interconnections.
- We should cultivate good images in our minds for the human and planetary future. These should express our role in creating this good future.

Held to with steadfastness and love, these ideas, actions, and imaginings will emerge in a true land ethic and as health and harmony in the real world of our grandchildren.

NOTES

1. Quoted in T. C. McLuhan, *Touch the Earth* (New York: Pocket Books, 1972), p. 56.
2. W. Timothy Gallway, *Inner Tennis: Playing the Game* (New York: Random House, 1976), p. 143.
3. Joe Paddock, *The Things We Know Best: An Oral History of Olivia, Minnesota, and Its Surrounding Countryside* (Olivia, MN: Book 200, 1976), p. 70.

· 5 ·

Some Psychological Aspects of Land Stewardship

AN armchair theorist of the good type will sympathize with a real farmer's financial griefs. The theorist may be very keen on some sort of soil-preservation practice he or she has studied or heard of, but may still confess that it is easy enough to propose that the farmer do this procedure or that procedure, but when your debts stare you in the eye and you still haven't arranged for next spring's seed, that makes a lot of difference. That is the confession of an intelligent, empathizing theorist. What he or she, however goodwilled, may not realize is that a farmer not only must look at the expense of any new environmental practice, but had better plan on receiving some negative reinforcement from the neighbors and townspeople as well. We need to realize that "negative reinforcement" is the great American sneer, the response to anyone who upgrades his or her philosophy.

When the drunk totters out of the highway tavern saying, "That's it! I am finally going to try AA!" his fellow-drunks laugh at him. When a silly woman finally decides to spend only 10 percent of her time being well dressed and 90 percent doing some work, her fellow shoppers and companions at the beauty shop don't praise the decision: they watch for, smiling, and comment on, her slippage in grooming. When two generations of farmers have cultivated straight up and down mild hills and the third plans to lay out contours and grassways, the neighbors laugh. When older people decide to write their memoirs instead of watching TV in the common rooms all afternoon, the others laugh at them. "Put a lot of sex in it!" they laugh.

As we look at psychological aspects of good land stewardship, therefore, we need to make a list of the actual experiences the new steward will find militating against his or her new ethic:

- Lack of know-how in the new practices;
- Extra expense, getting equipment for the job;
- Lack of experience in developing a network of people to help with this kind of soil management;
- The insecurity that any new procedure brings with it;
- Lack of approbation, or open sneering from neighbors—anything from gentle grins to bullying.

Of all the troubles, this last is the hardest to bear. I remember farmhands sneering at anyone who wouldn't stand in the field with flags while the spray-pilot made his runs with chemicals that cause leukemia. I remember the cool of the spray on my face, and feeling proud that I was out there to help guide the pilot. The whole thing had more panache than much of what we did in the field. Later we heard about the chemicals, but you weren't much if you couldn't take a few chemicals. We sneered. We sneered at the first contour plowman in our area—but only indirectly, since he had some support from the Extension people. The first organic fertilizer people were sneered at because they fell into that great category called Standing in the Way of Progress—along with the officer from the Food and Drug Administration who did not allow thalidomide in the United States.

We should believe the smart people who have said over and over again that any new ethic brought into a community by one of that community's members will bring some scorn to that brave person. Alexis de Tocqueville said it in *Democracy in America,* Shakespeare said it in *Coriolanus,* James Agee said it in "A Mother's Tale," Irving Janis said it in *Groupthink* (Boston: Houghton Mifflin, 1983) and Yi-Fu Tuan, describing how rural communities fight anyone whose ideas are lower—or higher—than the common denominator, said it in *Segmented Worlds and Self: Group Life and Individual Consciousness* (Minneapolis: University of Minnesota Press, 1983).

The sneering at or disrespect for someone's new ethic is not what most people think. It is not merely hatred of something different: it is a heartfelt dislike of sacrifice. An ethical person agrees to eschew certain short-term benefits, financial or romantic, in favor of some long-term goals. An ethical farmer (in a simple example) eschews growing profitable corn on the land occupied by shelter-belt trees or contoured grassways. If land stewardship ideas catch on in a given county, obviously people will feel pressured to go along with them. That means that everyone must move from the short-term gain sphere to a longer-term gain sphere. The rebellious feelings that show up as sneering are rebellion against short-term sacrifice.

Hidden slightly behind those feelings is another cause for alarm: what if everyone gets to reevaluating how we work and live? Once an idea is up for review (such as farming or community), it is no longer sacred. Anything can happen. When habits come up for appraisal—cool appraisal—they no longer have the ring of dogma. For example, it was the habit of men in western Minnesota in 1955 to "finish up fall work" by Thanksgiving. That meant plowing the fields black, and leaving that soil there to lift off and blow in the subsequent winter and spring winds. It was part of the holy work of farming, however. Women praised men for having what we called "clean" fields by Thanksgiving. It was something like the way men praised women for being wonderful cooks.

In ten years' time we all knew that plowing clean in the fall begged for snirt (blowing snow and dirt) in the spring and soil loss by the tons per acre. In ten years' time we had also learnt that fried food, and gravy made in the frying pan, and artificial gelatin salads full of sugar, and pie made with both sugar and grease were not good food. Yet fall plowing and heavy meals were part of our religion. Men and women praised one another for carrying them on. It takes a while for us to drive about on Sunday afternoons—checking postboxes, of course—and say, instead of "You got a good check, Jim!" (a good pattern of check-planting cornseed), "You got wonderful topsoil maintenance even on those high spots, Jim!"

The greatest psychological jump that grown people must make is to switch from a purely technical philosophy to an ethical philosophy. A technical philosophy says, My problem in both work and leisure is, what will work? How will I get good enough at the process to do it profitably? How much capital, of both time and money, do I need to keep this process going? The ethical philosophy says, I have gone through the first stage. I am technically proficient at some level. Now I want to think about *whether* to be doing this—or what else I *ought* to be doing—for the common good. The common good, to an ethically grown-up person, is both lateral and vertical, encompassing those physically and temporally far away.

The psychology of ethics is that it is the second step in people's lives, not the first. In our childhood and teens, and even in our twenties, most of us spend our energy in the technical stage—learning expertise with toys, work, housekeeping. It is our natural bent. The baby in her bassinet has breast or bottle offered. If she hears a baby in the next bassinet crying out of genuine starvation, the baby being fed certainly will not offer her milk supply to the hungry baby. The idea won't even cross her mind. When I was learning to drive a tractor, I stood on the bar and listened while my boss explained the gears and, in the case of that particular machine, what revolutions to keep her at. If you had come up to me during those ten minutes and told me that the tractor would compact soil and cause hardpan or that the spray I was dragging behind was poisonous to the microorganisms in the topsoil, I would have been nothing but scornful. My reality at that point was technical proficiency: *how,* not *whether.* That comes first, and as a stage of development, it can't be skipped. Everyone must start with simple technical interest in the world.

Rural society encourages us to stay in the technical stage rather long. We are all in accord on technical issues: they are mildly interesting and they don't cause religious or political fights at the supper table. As long as the conversation is about *how* to run the electric train on the Feast of St. Stephen or *how* to strike a field so there's no running over previously worked land—or even *how* to run a menu on a 40-column monitor—there are no arguments. Families unused to a lot of conversation, even downright shy people, can enjoy mild exchanges about how toys and machines and households are run. We needn't be surprised, therefore, that millions of people in all walks of life spend most of their lives in the technical stage of development. As members of a family, a neighborhood, a community, they find it the least painful modus vivendi possible.

Alas, it is also the most dangerous. Historically it has allowed people to do evil while scarcely noticing they are doing it. At the Nuremburg trials we heard mass murderers report that it was simply a job and they did it. They saw the genocide as a series of technical problems—how to obtain Zyklon-B gas despite U.S.A.F. bombing of railroad lines, and so forth.

The idealist likes to be shocked and to judge people who do evil as evil. More likely they are just stunted. They cannot get from the technical stage of psychic development to the ethical stage.

How do people get blocked from developing an ethic toward their life work—toward other people, toward the environment, toward the soil? How, exactly, is such stunting done?

First, let's look at some people who are not ethically blocked, and see whether the steps they take are difficult. Let's make up a farm couple who operate two sections of midwestern land. Gray and Jodie Anschau, let us say, have gone to get help redesigning their fields according to contour. They have made a plea against the neighboring farm corporation, whose methods cause rill erosion on Gray and Jodie's land. So far they aren't having much luck with the plea because the corporation is operating that land for a huge insurance company, which sees its responsibility as getting cash profit for its investors, not as maintaining the soil long-term. Other farm operators have told Gray and Jodie they will get nowhere against the insurance company operation.

Gray and Jodie have taken two steps that a merely technical person never takes: first, they have drawn apart from the rest of the group long enough to think and make up their own minds about what's right. Second, they have decided to take a stand although their peers' consensus is that it is hopeless. Both steps, withdrawing to think and deciding not to feel hopeless, are painful, self-realizing things to do.

Gray and Jodie no sooner took those two steps, however, than their awareness of meaning in life quadrupled. They traded in psychic ease for increased pain—and meaning. They asked themselves these questions:

- How do I *want* to treat the land—if I can swing it? (What actually is my attitude, if any, toward the soil itself? Not toward my corn plants, but toward the soil?)

- If we become land stewards, how much unpleasant reaction will we have to expect from neighbors and others?
- How hard will it probably be to get not just us but many, many others in our area to do the same?
- When—sooner? or later?—will we come smack up against the genuine enemies of land stewardship—that is, against not just people who need consciousness-raising about soil but people who benefit, perfectly consciously, from bad soil practices?
- And finally, saying that these enemies of good land stewardship for one reason or another do not drive us off our land or ruin us financially with their cunning, how many other ethical changes are we looking at in ourselves? Here we are, who once just farmed with such techniques as we knew, now farming with techniques *and* with a land ethic: how many other parts of our lives will change from just somehow doing the job to *thinking* and evaluating about the job?

To develop their interest in a land ethic, Gray and Jodie stood slightly apart from their colleagues in farming. They formed a loose network with some other people from neighboring counties. They went to a couple of land stewardship institutes in cities a hundred miles away. It was appropriate for them to draw away from the local community and to draw close to an idea network. But they cannot continue that way indefinitely. They need to stay close to their rural community. The armchair environmentalist typically underestimates how important it is for the person with a new ethic to stay very close, very involved, with the old townspeople and township people around. It is a psychological aspect of morality: if you change one moral idea, be sure to stay quite conventional about everything else—at least for a few years.

Gray and Jodie are therefore careful to go on bringing hot dishes to bereaved families. It is an old ethic of their community, and a good one. They are careful to take their turn at chairing the Golden Age Circle of the church, not just the circles whose members are Jodie's age. Gray shows up at seed-corn banquets in January and February and asks highly technical questions, after the film, about the new machinery being advertised by implement dealers. Jodie is careful to be supportive of old values (such as the caring bringing-up of children in the home, not at daycare centers) as well as of good new values (such as women's defining their own interests and careers). They don't want to become people always shrill about some new cause.

There is a little psychological disarray that follows right after a couple like Gray and Jodie begin to show their interest in land stewardship, as they redefine how they talk to each other in the home. Men and women in the technical stage tend to keep work talk divided from recreational talk. They talk work with people of their own sex and make small talk or jokes with people of the other sex. Once people move into the ethical stage, however, both men and women talk about ethical issues together. They tend to mix in serious mention of work at the dinner table because their work has become full of sharable meaning for them now. Since ideas are sharable even if two people have divided their farming into specialized areas—home and farmyard to her, shop and fields to him, for example—they still have much to talk about. When Gray and Jodie go to a New Year's Eve party, then, with six other couples who are still in the technical stage, those other couples will notice that Gray and Jodie exchange ideas. Jodie does not look to Gray to answer all conceptual questions asked. Gray does not expect to talk about ideas with the men only.

The impact will be felt. It is part of the psychology of land stewardship. True friends are people who feel themselves to be in the service of a cause larger than themselves. They have much to talk about: they compare notes on how well they are serving. They keep gauging the road ahead, celebrating the miles behind. C. S. Lewis, in *The Four Loves,* goes farther. He says that a friendship is weakened greatly by having mere maintenance of that friendship as its highest goal. It becomes just a sort of psychic tangle without grace—requiring a good deal of nervous monitoring. That kind of psychic tangle, however, is the kind of relationship much touted by present American culture. Most people would never guess the pure enjoyment shared by friends and lovers who are fellow workers in a serious ethic.

Apparently virtue is very interesting. Gray and Jodie enjoy comparing right use and wrong use of soil. They enjoy their conversations about it. Hour for hour, they talk more than other rural couples. The land stewardship ethic is an unmistakable psychological gift to friendship and marriage. In rural areas where farmers are aware of land ethics, the sociability is unmistakably more lovely than where men talk technical problems and women catch the habit from the men and tend to talk about child raising as if it were a technical problem.

Before leaving this cheerful psychological aspect of land ethic, I would like to examine what happens without it. Let us say that virtue is indeed very interesting and rather contagious. If that is so, then lack of virtue is comparatively boring. Let us say that lack of a land ethic makes farming more boring than having a land ethic. It makes the social exchanges around the house and community more boring, too. If life were boring, people's recreational habits would be oriented toward escape rather than toward philosophical reflection. Well, and is much of American recreational life escape-oriented? Through set TV programs and through mood-changing liquor and drugs? Yes, it is.

I think we need to say that if one's recreational habits are 100 percent escape, with no reflection on life among friends, one is exhibiting signs of ethical stunting. A common myth is that only a few of the human species care to be ethical and talk about ethical things. It is very likely a lie. Viktor Frankl, reporting about philosophical meditations he deliberately introduced in his barracks at Auschwitz, said that those conversations were life-giving to everyone. To say that some people haven't a love of philosophy and goodness and therefore may as well be drunk or sports-passive because it suits them is wrong. It is a psychological parallel to people saying, in the nineteenth century, that working-class English and Welsh children were suited for the seventeen-hour day of labor in the mines, whereas the children of gentlemen were not.

It is significant that the sociability of the Grays and Jodies in our countryside is expanding. We should take cheer at the incredible changes in communication that the last thirty years have brought to rural America. It has to do with people deciding to think about themselves and their lives' meaning.

A last word about our being naturally moral animals. When people see no particular morality to their work—that is, when they regard what they do as simply a practical set of procedures—those people, oddly enough, develop ultra-moral attitudes on some very strange subjects. It is as if we each have some quota of moral-thinking energy in us, and if we don't apply it to our work, we'll apply it around haphazardly in our avocations. To give some examples: in the 1970s among young people, many of the really idle beach-enjoyers, who were not in the antiwar movement or in the women's movement and did not do much work of any kind, were vociferous about the rightness of living on brown rice and the wrongness of eating steak. They were morally disgusted by polyester dresses and morally respectful of engineer-striped overalls. It is interesting that they regarded the macrobiotic diet not as healthy, but as virtuous. I have heard strongly felt arguments about hanging clothes out on the line in subfreezing weather as opposed to using the dryer. Careful listening shows that moral, not merely aesthetic or practical, energy informs the conversation. These examples suggest that virtuous feelings float about inside us, and if they do not come to a sensible harbor in our work they will make shore somewhere else—and we end up with quirks of virtue.

Before leaving ethical consciousness-raising behind and going on to consider a more painful part of land stewardship, I would like to bring out another point that an armchair environmentalist or moral theorist might not consider: farming, whether done wretchedly or sloppily or beautifully, happens to be interesting work. Its being out-of-doors, its having to do with at least three seasonal changes, its allowing the farmer to plan his or her own work, its sense of virtuous solitude—its blessed hours of separateness from mouthy humanity—all make it interesting. Even if one is farmhand to a sloppy operator, whose wrecked disks and chewed-out sty-timbers are dumped against the outbuildings, it is still a beautiful thing to arrive at the farm first thing in the morning and set your lunchbox into the tool bin of the tractor. Even if, because this is the 1980s and not the 1930s, *she* won't give you supper after a day's work, it is still a lovely thing to all clump into the cafe in town, crowd into a booth, and feel tiredness as if tiredness itself were an accomplishment.

The beauty of the fields, even if half their microorganisms are depleted by stupid side-dressings, and the tiredness of the day's work, even if it comes from a day of cultivating straight up and down balding slopes, give farming its interest. Farming, unlike labor, is so interesting in itself that those who do it sometimes put off making ethical decisions. The land itself still offers its wonderful life-style, and, alas, nothing stunts moral growth more than to be already enjoying a wonderful life-style. I add this observation so that when someone asks, "Can't that farmer see that rilling?" we know enough to say, "The farmer is seeing so much else that is beautiful, it could be seasons before he or she would see the rilling."

Last of all, let's take up the main enemy of a land ethic or any other ethic: that is, the people who benefit from the present poor behavior. Some people are genuine enemies of the land. They don't require consciousness-raising about the soil. They are perfectly conscious. They fully understand that their practice is depleting the soil. They do it because it works for them.

We need to think about enemies of the land. An enemy is anyone whose short-term goals are destructive of the long-term welfare of others. A comforting mistake made by thousands of idealists is to believe that if only all the world understood the gravity of soil erosion, all the world would want the abuse stopped. It is like the pathetic conviction of nineteenth-century Russian peasants that if only the Little Father (their pain-avoidance epithet for the Tzar) knew of their sufferings at the hands of bailiffs, finance cheats, and richer peasants, the Tzar would be righteously indignant on their behalf; he would, of course, do away with their enemies! What these artless people, the victims, did not grasp was that the Tzar's interests coincided in a workable way with the nobility's interests. They all took the baths in Germany together. What did the Tzar care if a few tens of thousands of peasants starved?

Idealists about soil depletion and land use need to grasp the unpleasant fact that land profiteers will oppose a land ethic wherever it has enough critical mass to interfere with their profits.

There are psychological categories that people fall into with respect to any ethic. It helps to list the categories, because each represents a mindset that operates on the ethic in question:

1. Those who first propose the ethic—the reformers.
2. Those who see life still as merely technical—who are passive and apathetic about good and bad.
3. Those who consciously break the ethic for now, who see themselves as practicing a little evil, but who mean to do

that only for a while. As soon as they are out of their current financial trouble, they intend to be ethical, even generous.

4. Those who regard themselves as unaffected by the particular ethic. They see the whole issue as not in their backyard, and therefore do not bother to formulate an opinion about it. They cheerfully feel themselves to be home free on this one.
5. The vicious few who care for no one but themselves, who mean to carry on unethically because it is profitable and who will bring adversarial measures to bear, if need be, to protect their interests.

Even paranoids generally agree that the truly vicious members of our species are few. Then why are they so effective? Someone else—people from one or more of the other four categories—must be doing their work for them. If that is so, we should check the categories and make intelligent guesses.

In at least a few cases, foolish idealists unwittingly do the work of the vicious few. Such people give time and money to causes that sound good at first. Many of us must have had a grandmother who supported America First because she wanted to further Lend-Lease and assist convoys of supplies to England. Idealists are at present visiting Nicaragua on both sides. Most likely they are not all clear about what Sandinistas stand for, what contras stand for.

It is probable that the best servants of the vicious few are passive members of groups two (technicians), three (temporary opportunists), and four (people detached from the issue, whose supporting votes can therefore be traded for). All of these passive people can be educated by public information. When their consciousness is appropriately raised, they may well stop being passive and adopt a good ethic—toward the land, if that is the context in which they are approached. I make a point of identifying these psychological mindsets so that we do not use the wrong instrument on the wrong kind of person. Idealists about land use may make technically minded people see soil use as right and wrong, they may use publicity to make those temporarily practicing bad soil use stop doing so sooner or immediately, they may make people on West 39th Street in New York understand that good soil stewardship does affect New Yorkers' well-being, too—but they will not convert the vicious few with information only.

I once attended a brilliant three-hour Crisis Management workshop at which the director demonstrated to our group of 200 or so how to bring an organization in trouble back to reexamining its original mission *before* the fur flew too hard. In the question period that followed, I asked how to use these crisis management principles when one of the contenders is a genuine jerk. Everyone laughed, but the director told us very flatly that crisis management—consciousness-raising along specific lines—does not work when one party is a jerk. In that case, she explained without levity, you need quite a different method. We understood that she meant an enemy is an enemy, and when communication in goodwill fails, one turns to adversarial approaches based on power.

Finally, then, who are the vicious few—so far as land stewardship is concerned? Natural enemies of the land include such real-estate interests as put the land into management by people who want quick returns from it. Natural enemies of the land are legislators who manipulate tax laws so that farm benefits go to large operators instead of small. Natural enemies of the land are those chemical concerns that reap a profit from saturating millions of farms with dangerous chemical residue, carefully advertising in such a way that their products appear to go hand-in-glove with good soil conservation. There are other natural enemies of the land, but our business here is not to identify every single opponent of a land ethic, but to identify our psychological attitudes about the ethic.

We need to do at least one thing that is painful: we need to admit that some people are indeed against a good land ethic. Their position is adversarial. Power is what we need to meet their salients: when they attack good land use through legislation or commercial leverage, we will have to defend the soil through legislation and commercial leverage. Consciousness-raising is appropriate only to the other groups, the unawakened and those who feel detached from the issue.

A cheerful conclusion: it is surprisingly easy to interest large numbers of Americans in issues they once thought irrelevant. The reason these people can be roused to good land stewardship, for example, even if they sell clothing on West 39th Street, is that human beings are as curious as cats. Human beings are immensely interested in the technical details of other people's lives. The North Carolina woods are full of retired North Carolinians who are very well read on Viking side-ruddering of ships. At any one time there are thousands of little boys and girls who know a *Spitfire Mark II* from a *Spitfire Mark III*, although both models have been out of use since 1945 and the children will likely never see them in flight. They're just plain interested. I once got into a conversation with a skilled black-marketeer who had made a fortune off his army experiences in North Africa. He spent a full half-hour intensely involved in the difference between the needlepoint "half cross" stitch and the needlepoint "continental" or "tenting" stitch: he was fascinated by the different involvement of yarn on the back side of the work. There are quiet women in New Mexico who become immersed in how a spencer can be used to keep a sailing ship nosed upwind throughout a bad storm. People even love one another's jargon. University instructors pick up on "down corn" and farmers pick up on "inloading lecture schedules."

This human curiosity and love of someone else's particulars can be counted on to help with making a land ethic popular in America. Our advertising of land stewardship should always include a small technical tableau for the reader or watcher. The sharing of technical details, just the tiniest detail, is the basis that will bring all sorts of people into an ethical fellowship with the land.

We must make canny use of the insight that when people know several technical particulars about someone or something outside their own world, they feel affectionate toward that someone or something. If, for example, you teach city people, just as a symbol, exactly what is involved in turning a cultivator in the headlands (and explain about the headlands) that city person will imagine himself or herself doing it. The city person will imagine being up there on the tractor, watching out for all the little plants. He or she will see the neat darkness of the soil, and the incredible delicacy of the drilled corn, new pale green as floppy as babies' fingers. The next time the city person drives past a cornfield, there will be an affectionate identity. Then—step two: when that city person hears about a land ethic, the response will not be indifference or cynicism. For if we are as curious as we obviously are about one another's technical problems, we are latently a thousand times more curious about one another's ethical considerations.

· 6 ·

The Uses of Beauty:

FARMLAND AESTHETICS IN THE TWENTIETH CENTURY

OFTEN, while driving westward toward Brookings, South Dakota, I am moved by a feeling of warmth and protectedness created by several miles of well-established windbreaks. I am moved also by the beauty of that landscape. One senses here a considerable enhancement of ecological complexity: a highly productive agriculture coexists, not only with long, soil-protecting arms of trees and brush, but also with the wildlife they shelter and feed. My sense of pleasure in driving through these protected miles is, however, diminished by an awareness of the immense reaches of surrounding farmland that are not so protected. On our northern prairies, winter winds scour thousands of square miles of fall-plowed fields till the snow turns black. The occasional winding line of jackrabbit or coyote tracks, as one senses the harshness of circumstances in which these animals must survive, only adds to the pervading chill. In such a landscape, the eye that hungers for beauty must be sharp:

> In a county ninety-seven percent under
> the plow, we find beauty in the skinny
> ribbon of orange and amber grass
> that waves, unmowed,
> between the road and the ruler's edge
> of a plowed field.

> We find beauty in the shine
> inside an empty milkweed pod,
> and in the creek,
> that wanders within its naked
> straightened banks.
>
> Nancy Paddock,
> "We Find Beauty"

As within, so without. Our inner selves are expressed on and in the land we control. I have been told that, under the influence of the Thatcher government, the ancient field hedges of England are being torn out to make way for an American-style industrial agriculture. Fifteen years ago, as this form of agriculture was beginning to crest on our midcontinental prairies, farmers bulldozed windbreaks planted in response to the Dust Bowl experience of the 1930s. Internally, the owners of this land—and their advisers—had reduced their values to those of short-term economic efficiency, and this barrenness has been visited upon the land. Over much of America it is the background for the lives of rural people.

Those who design modern agriculture, though they might claim for themselves the "aesthetics" of efficiency, would have us look elsewhere for beauty. These designers no doubt consider nonutilitarian demands extraneous, perhaps even frivolous and irresponsible. Such thinking, however, ignores the fundamental truth that health and beauty are in large part synonymous. When we consider that 50 percent of our erosion occurs on 10 percent of our farmland, the portion that is considered *marginal*, it should be obvious that the development (or redevelopment) of aesthetic feeling for land in agrarian America could and should be a truly important "tool" for conservation of soil.

Marginal land is usually hilly and in other ways diversified, and when left alone, is beautiful. Given the thesis, as we argued in chapter three, that overproduction has become the major economic problem for farmers, a strong case can be made for allowing marginal lands to return to a state of beauty and stability. Winter trips to tropical paradises may be nice, but it is sad that the beauty of our own land has been sacrificed to make such trips possible.

On the other hand, there are many landholders who, though successful farmers, do find a place for the aesthetic on their land and in their lives. In an oral interview, a Catholic cultural worker, Sister Mary Mark Tacheny, of St. Paul, told me of one such landholder:

> A while back, a farmer from southern Minnesota came to one of our board meetings to share some slides he had taken of his farm. He had just been named conservationist of the year in his region. He had maybe eight or ten slides. Shots he had taken himself of wooded land and a marsh right outside his breakfast nook. Shots of wildflowers and of birds in the marsh. Then he had a couple of how he had guarded the land right outside this area to keep it from washing. He had put in a terrace.
>
> "These are right outside the place where I have breakfast in the morning," he said. "My wife and I can eat our breakfast in this beautiful space."
>
> He showed these pictures with such love and reverence that he had our entire group in a prayerful attitude. It was meditation time. The biggest exploiter would almost have been brought to his knees, because of the reverence and respect with which this farmer told the story of his farm. His most important point was that this woodlot was terribly important to him, and there was nothing in all the world that would cause him to cut down those trees and plow up the ground for a few acres of cropland. If we could just get more folks to have that kind of appreciation for what a particular piece of land is best suited.[1]

Landowners, with few exceptions, love the natural beauty of their land. As hunters, or simply observers, they love, too, the wildlife that land in its natural condition expresses. Contemporary agricultural values have, however, increasingly caused landowners to suppress this love in favor of a narrow practical relationship with their land. In recent years, with monotonous regularity, the back pasture with its groves has been sacrificed to the plow and the bulldozer; the marshland has been drained. Evening walks, serenity, the contemplation of natural beauty have been sacrificed—first, in the hope of increased economic reward, then in the name of economic survival. The return on these actions has not, of course, been economic well-being, but a barren landscape.

To the degree that we reduce our relationship to farmland to its utilitarian aspects, we lose contact with a larger set of assets and liabilities that would help us to maintain holistic well-being. The short-term, resource-management approach to farmland leaves us at the mercy of the infantile impulses of personal greed: the sticky hand reaching for yet another ice-cream cone, inhibited only by the bellyaches of overconsumption. By taking a larger view of our landscape, by breathing with it, enjoying its health and beauty (or suffering in the lack of these), we extend greatly the base from which we make our land-use decisions.

When we consider farmland aesthetics, picture postcard beauty is but one possibility. Aldo Leopold made clear that, for the more advanced levels of aesthetic perception, we must learn to see through the surface of things. The geological, the ecological, the human past can be read in the landscape of the present. In a poem titled "Black Energy," I once attempted to catch this sense of the past as it is implied by the life in a healthy soil:

Life is seething in this soil
which has been millions of years
in the making.
It has been forever
in the making.

A mingling of everything
which ever whistled here, leaped
or waved in the wind.
Plants and animals,
grasses of this prairie.
Buffalo and antelope grazing down
into roots and back again
into the sun.
Birds and insects, their wings still hum
in this soil.

And this swarm drinks
sunlight and rain,
and rises again and again
into corn and beans
and flesh and bone.

The quick bodies of animals and men
risen
from this black energy.[2]

Many who work in soil conservation have been struck by how one's aesthetic response to the soil changes with knowledge. Until the very recent past, for example, when talking of fall plowing, farmers "turned her black." And this newly turned soil was looked at with pride, was thought beautiful. The occasional uncovered bit of crop residue, corn or bean stalk, was a blemish, was called "trash." Recently, however, conservation-minded people have come to realize that "trash" left evenly over the surface of farmland through the winter months controls both wind and water erosion. With this recognition, little by little, they have come to see this residue as beautiful. Conservation farmer Milo Hanson once told me: "I have now come to the point where if I see a totally black field I get sick. I feel good now only when I see a real messy field that's *just covered* with crop residue."

What we know does make an enormous difference in our aesthetic response to the land. If the corn is tall and laden with ears but the groundwater beneath it has been tested unfit to drink, our sense of beauty is also poisoned. In one who loves the earth and is sensitive to its needs, the lifeless and chalky quality of soil that has been diminished by years of erosion and chemical farming calls up visions of starvation and the desert. Healthy soil, on the other hand, of the sort that one finds, say, under leaf mold in the woods—moist and rich in humus and seething with microorganisms, worms, and insects—promises bountiful life. As any serious gardener can testify, such soil stirs an aesthetic excitement in us. We long to get our hands into it, to merge with it and its fruits.

The great soil scientist Hans Jenny carries this idea even further:

> Soil appeals to my senses. I like to dig in it and work it with my hands. I enjoy doing the soil texture feel test with my fingers or kneading a clay soil, which is a short step from ceramics or sculpture.

Jenny sees something like great abstract art in the spectrum of colors in a soil profile:

> In loess country, plowed fields on slopes show wide bands of attractive color gradations from dark browns to light yellows, caused by erosion of the surface soil. Warm brownish colors characterize fields and roofs in

> Cezanne's landscape paintings of southern France, and radiant red soils of the tropics dominate canvasses of Gauguin and Portinari. Soil profiles viewed in pits may reveal vivid color and structure patterns of layers and horizons. I have seen so many delicate shapes, forms, and colors in soil profiles that, to me, soils are beautiful.[3]

Utilitarian planners may claim that we now need soil only to hold plant roots in place while we provide artificial nutrients, but the individual who has an aesthetic sense for soil hears in such talk only an invitation to the wasteland.

As we look through the surface of things, we soon realize that aesthetic power lives in the land—not only in the visual sense, but in the dramatic as well. For those who have eyes to see, each tongue of life—be it worm, wheat plant, June bug, or browsing deer—tells a perfect tale. Which ends in death. Over and over again.

When we have lived with a piece of ground for a long time, the drama of its human past also becomes a living presence for us. The European immigrant left his sacred earth behind when he came to this new land, but we now have many "hundred-year farms" that our great-grandparents watered with their sweat. The limitations of their time left them little choice but to dwell in continuous contact with their land, and they knew it intimately. Memories, stories from this past now live in our minds. Because we know them, we know, too, ourselves.

In the middle seventies, I had a conversation with a seemingly sensitive young man who held pride in being the operator of a farm first settled by his great-grandfather. As he talked it became clear that he was suffering because he had recently torched a living family museum: the abandoned house, with its surrounding grove, that his grandfather had built and in which his father had been born. Several times he listed for me the game animals the grove had sheltered: deer, raccoon, rabbits, pheasant, squirrels. As a small boy, he had "run wild" there too, as had his children, and they cried when he destroyed it. His lender, he told me, had pressured him for several years to gain that extra eight acres of farmland.

Such deeds were the farmland ethos of that time, and his anxious language abounded with the platitudes of efficiency and growth. Before he bulldozed and burned the house and timber, he took photographs. He showed them to me. I could see only surfaces in them. He, of course, could see volumes. His emotions seemed complex: shame and a slight sense of horror for what he had done, but shame, too, that his emotions were so strong.

In my interview with Sister Mary Mark Tacheny, she told me of a farm family that at the birth of each new child had planted a tree somewhere on its ground. Such a symbolic bonding with the life of its land must surely have made that family feel a part of its ongoing "story." In ways such as this, little by little, a new land becomes the land of our mothers and fathers, becomes our sacred ground. Utilitarian industrial agriculture, however, has diminished such family bonding with the land. Our next generation may scarcely know it.

Wendell Berry, perhaps our country's most powerful exponent of traditional agriculture and sound land stewardship, describes our bonding with land through the metaphor of marriage. He has, in fact, written a book of poetry entitled *The Country of Marriage* (San Diego: Harcourt Brace Jovanovich, 1973). Though he has produced perhaps more prose than poetry, even Berry's prose is informed and controlled by an exquisite poetic sense. The title of another of his books of poetry, *Farming: A Hand Book* (San Diego: Harcourt Brace Jovanovich, 1970) was a stroke of genius. This practical-sounding title reminds us of the usefulness of those dimensions of agriculture that are not immediately utilitarian. It may be that no one else has ever so clearly and passionately described the aesthetic content of farming. "The Man Born to Farming," the opening poem of *Farming: A Hand Book*, is typical of his work:

> The grower of trees, the gardener, the man born to
>   farming,
> whose hands reach into the ground and sprout,
> to him the soil is a divine drug. He enters into death
> yearly, and comes back rejoicing. He has seen the
>   light lie down
> in the dungheap, and rise again in the corn.
> His thought passes along the row ends like a mole.
> What miraculous seed has he swallowed
> that the unending sentence of his love flows out of
>   his mouth
> like a vine clinging in the sunlight, and like water
> descending in the dark?

There is nothing, of course, in the modern "ag" textbook that communicates the aesthetic dimensions of farming. These have, in fact, been denied. If someone were to tiptoe into the contemporary "ag" classroom and read Wendell Berry's poem, and it were truly heard, everything would have to stop. Everything would have to be rethought. The ignition to the immense four-wheel-drive tractor would have to be switched off. The operator would take from his head the earphones blaring rock and country music into his brain. Blinking, he would come down his little ladder and plant his feet on the ground, kick at it, take a look around. Such, in truth, has been the effect of Wendell Berry's work on the occasional individual who was ready to hear him. But most of our "ag" schools and farmers have not as yet even heard of him. Nor, sad to say, have half of this country's soil professionals.

Inherent in prose, I believe, is a dilemma to which poetry (all art) is the answer. Communicating in prose, as we do, trapped in the prosaic levels of life, we can only intuit wholeness. We yearn, but we cannot break from the linear ruts of the rational; and modern life, hungering for the soul, withers on its vine. When writing poetry, we allow in the wholeness, we welcome it. We work with images and rhythms capable of conveying, of carrying, wholeness. The reader or listener is in turn given an experience of wholeness, a moment in time that is complete, one in which he or she does not feel the need to change or control the world. When and if our lives ever express our wholeness—our *poetry*—we will know harmony with the land. Such, indeed, was the case with many traditional cultures that survived in harmony for thousands of years, until overrun by our own in its hunger for growth and change.

The forms of communication of utilitarian, chem-tech agriculture, like those of war, squeeze hard to eliminate any glimmerings of poetry. They may even be best described by their lack of poetry. When attempting to sell the public, however, industrial agriculture does not do so with fact sheets and chemical tables. In its advertising, industrial agriculture uses the feeling modes of art and poetry to convince us of its worth. And, miracle of miracles, for a few brief aesthetic moments, the wholeness of the old vision of farming is flashed across the television screen to convince us of the value of the new. It is perverse that modern agriculture seeks acceptance through association with what it destroys. Art, music, and poetry were once considered to be the hallmarks of a culture's connection with truth and beauty. It seems likely, as is often suggested, that today mainstream America is best expressed by its advertising art. This should give us pause.

Wendell Berry's poetic expression of our marriage with the earth leads to the notion of husbandry, a cocreativeness that is more artistic than scientific. Like the artist, the husband to the land makes many particular and individualized decisions as he responds to the specific needs of each acre he works. Industrial agriculture, on the other hand, seeks, through chemical additives and the power of its machines, to homogenize the land. In resisting such an approach, true husbandry carries with it a load of feeling, of poetry, which confounds the idea of Earth as the ground floor of a production factory.

The aesthetic/creative pleasures of husbandry—the perception of beauty and meaning in the processes of working with the land—are mature ones. Youth loves a virgin Earth, with possibilities of unspoiled richness on into infinity. In youth, the first symptoms of wear signal, not the need for husbandry, but that it's time to move on. Youth believes in the horizon, beyond which a new green valley, untouched and wonderfully fertile, lies forever waiting. With, however, all the new green valleys of Earth now plowed and eroded, the vigor of our youthful relationship with it depends increasingly on new layers of technology. With these, though the beauty of Earth may be diminished, the promise of everlasting abundance continues.

In both our individual and collective lives, however, there comes a time, early in maturity, when we want to give back, to build back. This is due in part to the experience of age in our own flesh. We now recognize limits in ourselves and, by extension, the world. The shock of recognition is painful, but, as the Chinese book of wisdom, *I Ching*, tells us, there is good fortune to be had in working on what has been spoiled. This should cheer us in our efforts to husband the plenty that remains. Things are perhaps not quite what we would have them be, but, just as the aging husband in a human marriage accepts and continues to love and honor the aging body of his wife, those who husband land must continue to love and maintain what has been diminished. We must never forget that what is worn—the silvered and fallen barn, the wrinkled face, and yes, even the eroded field—carries a message with deep spiritual meaning. We must not turn from it.

Unless we make the shift from youthful self-indulgence to mature and responsible husbandry, the second half of life is no more than a sad waning toward death. But, if we can make it through this passage, we will find beauty and joy in our cocreative involvement with the ingredients of life: the weather, the seasons, the soil, and the seed opening up into light and harvest.

A major part of our reward will come in knowing that we have not, in these processes, diminished the earth. And its health and well-being will be our own. It may be that Western culture is now, collectively, experiencing enough "pain in its flesh" to force that step toward maturity that will open for us the aesthetic pleasures of husbandry. This should, in turn, ensure for us that the earth, though at present somewhat worn, will be maintained at a level of health that will allow the continuance of human civilization.

Aesthetic experience has less to do with effort than with openness. To experience the land aesthetically one must give up the struggle to dominate it, and instead become receptive to its beauty and its drama. It is then that we merge, that we lose ourselves in the deep truth of our oneness with the whole. As many an artist has found, there is nothing greater than to be alive in the creation, to have eyes and ears to experience it, to be able to participate in its processes. Anyone who lives on and with the land, who works with its forces, also has access to these aesthetic experiences. The individual who has opened to them is proof against willing participation in the rampaging destruction of the natural world that has so characterized our century.

NOTES

1. Joe Paddock, from transcript of unpublished interview with Sr. Mary Mark Tacheny, St. Paul, MN, 1984.
2. Joe Paddock, "Black Energy," in *Earth Tongues* (Minneapolis: Milkweed Editions, 1985), p. 43.
3. Hans Jenny, interview in "My Friend the Soil," *Journal of Soil and Water Conservation*, May–June 1984, p. 15.

· II ·

Standing in The Center of The World

· 7 ·

Myths, Dreams, Heroes

THE root system of a large and beautiful tree in its downward spread may be equal to the upward spread of its leaves and branches. We tend not to be conscious of the underground tree, but its importance is equal to that of what has risen into air and sunlight. In a similar sense, when we observe human works in the outer world, we are seldom aware of the inner psychic constructs from which they have risen.

The great mythologist Joseph Campbell, in his book *Primitive Mythology,* describes myths as the great releasers and channelers of human energy. Christ, for instance, or Gandhi or Hitler or modern advertisers, using the image language of myths, have released the flood of human energy in specific directions. "Clearly," writes Campbell, "mythology is no toy for children. Nor is it a matter . . . of archaic merely scholarly concern, of no moment to modern men of action. For its symbols . . . touch and release the deepest centers of motivation, moving literate and illiterate alike, moving mobs, moving civilizations."[1]

In considering how our inner lives affect our care of land, it will be useful to broaden our discussion to include heroes, hero worship, and our personal dreams and goals. These too are tied to the power of myth and its archetypal symbols. Images that express our goals and the personal qualities we most admire and desire are the models on which we, consciously or unconsciously, mold ourselves and the world around us.

The stories, with their "heroes," told in the Judeo-Christian tradition have functioned as myth in the sense we have been describing. As we shall see more fully in the next chapter, many believe that elements of the Judeo-Christian tradition have allowed a damaging relationship with the natural world. Very early in Genesis (1:27–28), for instance, humankind is given dominion over the land: "So God created man in his own image, in the image of God created he him; male and female created he them. And God blessed them, and God said unto them, be fruitful, and multiply, and replenish the earth, and subdue it; and have dominion over the fish of the sea, and over the fowl of the air, and over every living thing that moveth upon the earth."

Those heroes of Western culture who have for the moment gained control over the land did not have to look far for their justification. Having so easily found it, however, they must have quickly closed the Book, for much of the rest of the Old Testament and the example of Christ in the New abound with admonitions that we not abuse our dominion.

Early on in America's history, the Puritan tradition, centered in New England, was a powerful force in shaping the nation's expression of Christianity. Puritans in colonial settlements dreamed an otherworldly dream. They were in this world, but not of it. They saw themselves as the children of Israel, lost in the wilderness, looking for the promised land where they would build the heavenly city. Wilderness was of the devil—hideous, chaotic, and desolate—and they were in a constant struggle with it; first to survive, and then to create a civilization like the one they knew, where none at all had been. Wilderness, for the Puritan, was the enemy to be vanquished.

This vision of the land, at least in its natural state, as being actually evil, gave great energy to the Puritan community in crusading against it. And even though our farmland has most certainly now been tamed, even down to its underlying clay, we find it difficult to honor what had so recently been the enemy. As Wendell Berry has observed, however, the innate fertility of the soil is the wilderness within it, and in subjugating it we have clearly arrived at the point of diminishing returns. These arguments enable one to see a connection between Puritanism and the production and use of chemical fertilizers. The ancient plants and animals that are the source of most of this petroleum-based fertilizer have been "civilized," purified, and "Puritanized" through industrial processes.

Most of us no longer say grace. Those who do, tend simply to thank God and to forget the land, the farmer, and others involved in bringing food to our table. Not saying grace indicates that we no longer sense our sacred connection—or any connection—with the soil. It may be, too, that abundance—even excess—has brought us to a point where we are not particularly thankful for our food. In the seemingly greater logic of ancient history, abundant crops meant prosperity and well-being. Today they may mean the opposite.

In the distant past, numerous agricultural rituals, both Christian and "pagan," were a continuous reminder of human interdependence with the land. In Swedish tradition, for example, the last sheaf of grain harvested was considered to have magical power, to contain the generative essence of life itself. It was often fed to the birds—a giving back to nature—or it was saved and fed to cattle on Christmas morning or placed outside the house to bless those who lived or visited there. Such symbolic expressions and reminders of our connection to the land would be lost on most of us today.[2]

In the United States, until recently, the harvest itself—especially the threshing of small grain—was experienced by our largely agrarian populations as a major event. It was a time when neighborhoods came together in a mythic celebration of mutual interdependence, working and feasting in the joy of another harvest achieved. Oral history interviews abound in praise of this "celebration." It was the high point of the yearly agricultural cycle: "Yah, yah, them thrashin' days are gone away from me now. I wish to God I could turn back to them!"[3]

There is almost nothing in the life of urban industrial America that calls to mind the mystery and wonder of our food risen yet again from the ground. In fact, this sense has tended to vanish even from agriculture itself.

In the late nineteenth and the twentieth century, the dominant myths of Western civilization, especially in the United States, have tended to be more secular than sacred. In chapter four we described the powerful influence of the "frontier myth" on the development of our national character. B. A. Botkin, in *A Treasury of American Folklore,* extends this idea:

> A composite picture of the American hero would show him to be a plain, tough, practical fellow, equally good at a bargain or a fight, a star-performer on the job and a hell-raiser off it, and something of a salesman and a

> showman, with a flair for prodigious stories, jokes, and stunts and a general capacity for putting himself over. Our nearest approach to a national myth, explaining and justifying the many contradictions in our heroes, is the frontier or pioneer myth. This reconciles the primitive virtues of brute strength, courage, and cunning with the economic virtues of thrift, hard work, and perseverance.[4]

This "nearest approach to a national myth" describes, not a nature-sensitive type seeking harmony with the land, but a practical, no-nonsense individual who has power and enjoys expressing it. His dominion over the American land took the quickest, most "efficient" means available.

Then there is our belief, likewise secular, that any American can rise to the top of the ladder of success: the Horatio Alger myth. Another folklorist, Richard M. Dorson, in *America in Legend,* has written about this aspect of our national character:

> Americans do not see themselves as oppressed members of a working class, and union members do not identify with proletarian types in radical songs. Rather they buy the American dream of the free individual who, given a fair shake, may well make it to the top. The worker on the assembly line has not inspired ballads or legends. Indeed, a factory does not generate heroic lore as did the cattle trail, lumber camp, mining camp, oil field, or enginehouse, for there is nothing potentially heroic in turning a wrench. Charlie Chaplin in *Modern Times* epitomized the degradation of the assembly-line robot. American folklore has chosen to celebrate the master workman in the pioneering days of the extractive and transportation industries, at the same time that the mass culture extolled Carnegie, Rockefeller, and Ford as self-made men, flinty individualists, creating industrial empires in a wide open America through their initiative, dedication, and drive. The master workman and the empire builder stood on adjacent rungs of the American ladder of success.[5]

It may be that originally the Horatio Alger myth was stronger in urban areas than rural, but, as we argued in chapter three, this image has over the last generation or two become perhaps the dominant theme in American agriculture. The myth of the modest family farm, not overreaching itself, in balance within its complex sustaining forces, was passed over in favor of the dream of making it big, of adding acre to acre, farm to farm.

Puritan Christianity, the frontier, and Horatio Alger myths help explain the direction industrial agriculture has taken in the twentieth century. Just as Puritans once saw the wilderness as evil, many environmentalists now see this cluster of myths as evil. One might argue, however, that in the evolution of a people, myths emerge in response to the needs of a specific time. These three earlier myths gave pioneers the energy necessary to "tame" this continent, and no one can deny that it was their destiny to do so. Now that the taming has been accomplished, however, here and almost everywhere else, this particular combination of myths has become increasingly dangerous to the planet, including its human inhabitants.

I once heard a professor of paleontology tell a story about a certain prehistoric species of deer. The evidence, as laid down in the soil-become-rock of the immensely distant past, showed that this deer had become increasingly abundant with the growth of its antlers. At a certain point, however, apparently its antlers became so massive as to be a hindrance to its life, and its fossilized record appears nowhere in subsequent layers of rock. I find this story a metaphor for what might follow the current burgeoning of human technology. It may also suggest the eventual result of our continued and even growing adherence to myths that are no longer useful, as they were when we were struggling to gain a foothold in nature.

As certain writers have noted, in Western civilization there has always been an undercurrent of resistance to the dominant theme of exploitation. In fact, for a time at least, the most powerful myth of nineteenth-century America was that this continent was the "garden of the world," the "new Eden." This myth of the garden was especially powerful in the post-frontier period, when a nurturant agrarian tradition followed swiftly in the wake of the land-busting pioneer. Settlements were often named Eden, Eden Prairie, or Eden Valley. Orchards and vegetable and flower gardens were harmoniously arranged about the ideal farmsite of the period, and those farmsites bustled with life. Numerous outbuildings sheltered pigs and cattle, poultry, and horses. Modest acreages, fertilized by the livestock, sustained relatively complex rotations of food and feed grains. Much of the early farm was left in pasture and woodlots. There was need for many hands, and families were large. For a moment, at least, it seemed that the image of the garden was in control.

The modern mind, however, has found the machine more fascinating than the garden, and the title of a twentieth-century book by Leo Marx, *The Machine in the Garden,* tells the tale of our recent "fall." Old outbuildings now house machines and chemicals or are allowed to sink back into the ground. In the main, the farm family is fed from the supermarket like the rest of us. Extensive fields often produce but a single crop—a highly erosive one, planted in rows. There may be new metal buildings and a confinement operation for cattle or pigs or poultry. Expensively automated, such farms may or may not provide a living for one full-time operator. Most of the children leave home and seek education and employment in urban areas. On front lawns, TV satellite disks have begun to emerge like toadstools, homing devices for the images of the materialistic mythology of our time.

But what we need is new myths or reinterpretations of old ones that will channel our energies into socially and ecologically benign activities. A harmoniously balanced agricultural future, for instance, demands that we envision a farmer who can and will sustain such a future. As we assert throughout this book, we do not believe that a corporate planning committee or the farmer as businessman and technician can and will satisfy our needs for long-term sustainability. Over against the huge profit-oriented farms and ultra high-tech approaches that describe the future of industrial agriculture, Wendell Berry has set up an ideal based on the traditional European agriculture originally practiced in this country. This ideal farmer is rich in the lore of the past. His personal aims are modest. His goal is health throughout the interconnecting systems within which he works. He is a nurturer, not an exploiter.

Later we will see how the women's movement suggests ways in which we might better relate to the land. In describing his ideal farmer as a nurturer, Berry moves close to one strand of the feminist tradition. In fact, he argues that the true farmer must be able to move between what in Western society have traditionally been considered the male and female roles:

> It seems likely that all the "movements" of recent years have been representing various claims that nurture has to make against exploitation. The women's movement, for example, when its energies are most accurately placed, is arguing the cause of nurture; other times it is arguing the right of women to be exploiters—which men have no right to be. The exploiter is clearly the prototype of the "masculine" man—the wheeler-dealer whose "practical" goals require the sacrifice of flesh, feeling, and principle. The nurturer, on the other hand, has always passed with ease across the boundaries of the so-called sexual roles. Of necessity and without apology, the preserver of seed, the planter, becomes midwife and nurse. Breeder is always metamorphosing into brooder and back again. Over and over again, spring after spring, the questing mind, idealist and visionary, must pass through the planting to become nurturer of the real. The farmer, sometimes known as husbandman, is by definition half mother; the only question is how good a mother he or she is. And the land itself is not mother or father only, but both. Depending on crop and season, it is at one time receiver of seed, bearer and nurturer of young; at another, raiser of seed-stalk, bearer and shedder of seed. And in response to these changes, the farmer crosses back and forth from one zone of spousehood to another, first as planter and then as gatherer. Farmer and land are thus involved in a sort of dance in which the partners are always at opposite sexual poles, and the lead keeps changing: the farmer, as seed-bearer, causes growth; the land, as seed-bearer, causes the harvest.[6]

To these aspects of Wendell Berry's ideal farmer, I would suggest a complementary configuration. Though this farmer's feet will be planted in traditional European agriculture, he or she will be an ecosystem-person who, having increased access to information, will know of approaches to food production from all over the planet. He or she will be contemplative with a strong spiritual and aesthetic appreciation for the land. The farmer's technology may be traditional, may even in specific circumstances "go back to the horse," but it will also include a high (and benign) solar technology.

This farmer will have a deep understanding of the living environment, especially that which includes his or her farm. Most of the energy and fertility that powers this farm will rise from the workings of its immediate ecosystem. The control of life forms, insects and "weeds," that compete with food plants and animals will also, for the most part, depend on this farmer's deep understanding of ecological exchanges. Increasingly, the agro-ecosystem within which this farmer works will approach the qualities of a natural ecosystem. His or her ideals will be the same as those that have empowered the no-till agriculture of the Japanese farmer Masanobu Fukuoka; the intensive polycultural food-producing and living systems of New Alchemy in Wood's Hole, Massachusetts; and the mixed perennial permacultures of the Land Institute in Salina, Kansas, all of which are discussed in chapter fourteen, on ecoculture.

In our struggle to survive, we creatively strengthen the content of the myths that sustain us. We also continue to develop new myths and images that can buoy us in our efforts. John Todd, one of the principal originators of New Alchemy Institute, states that he has been interested in the power of symbols for some time.[7] He suggests that we develop eco-symbols that will inspire humanity as much as have, say, the high-tech symbols of space travel. New Alchemy has itself, it might be argued, become one such symbol, but Todd and his coworkers have also been working to design beautiful and efficient planetary stewardship sailing ships. These symbolic ships would course the globe carrying people capable of tackling difficult ecological problems; carrying, too, cargoes of trees, food plants, and marine animals that would be useful to indigenous populations and healing to specific ecosystems. Such a fleet of sailing ships, at once symbolic and practical, truly would catch in the winds of our collective imagination.

The Gaia hypothesis, as formulated recently by James Lovelock and Lynn Margulis, combines scientific ecological awareness with the Greek concept of Gaia, the Earth. This hypothesis suggests that not just the land, but our entire planet expresses the characteristics of a single living organism. Whatever its scientific accuracy, it has given us a new and useful myth that has captured the imagination of many and might substantially enhance our future relationship with the planet.

Finally, as we argue in chapter thirteen, "Food Production in the New Paradigm," the interconnected ecosystem itself may have emerged as a mythic symbol or model with the power to supplant the machine as our dominant model for reality. This would help to usher in what many are already calling the post-industrial world. If prevailing myths do emerge from a people in response to the needs of their time, we can be certain that, whatever its content, an entire constellation of healing imagery is now struggling to be born from our collective imagination.

NOTES

1. Joseph Campbell, *Primitive Mythology* (New York: Viking Press, 1970), p. 12.
2. Lilly Lorenzen, *Of Swedish Ways* (Minneapolis: Gilbert Publishing, 1964), pp. 210–11.
3. Joe Paddock, *The Things We Know Best* (Olivia, MN: Book 200, 1976), p. 62.
4. B. A. Botkin, *A Treasury of American Folklore* (New York: Outlet Book, 1984), pp. 2–3.
5. Richard M. Dorson, *America in Legend* (New York: Pantheon, 1973).
6. Wendell Berry, *The Unsettling of America* (San Francisco: Sierra Club Books, 1978), p. 8.
7. John Todd, "The Practice of Stewardship," in Wes Jackson, Wendell Berry, and Bruce Colman, eds., *Meeting the Expectations of the Land* (Berkeley, CA: North Point Press, 1984), p. 159.

·8·

Dust to Dust:

LAND IN THE JEWISH AND CHRISTIAN TRADITIONS

> In the sweat of your face
> you shall eat bread
> till you return to the ground,
> for out of it you were taken;
> you are dust
> and to dust you shall return.
> *Genesis 3:19*

THIS is the curse with which the Creator banished Adam and Eve from the garden into the perpetual work of agriculture. That we must sweat for bread is perhaps less hard for us to accept than that we have been consigned to dust. How can the exalted human being—little less than angel—be no more than dust on the wind? As if to resist this fate, civilization has constructed elaborate barriers against not only death but also reentry into the cycle of life. Some of us consign our bones to crypts guaranteed to last a thousand years. And Christian theology splits spirit from nature, promising divine redemption and the resurrection of the body at the end of time.

The dust from which we rise and into which we sink again, the dust from which we take great pains to separate ourselves, is, of course, soil. But some theologians are beginning to accept and celebrate their earthliness, transforming the curse into a blessing. "Dust to dust," restated slightly, becomes an affirmation of our communion with all life: "You are soil, and to soil you shall return." In this new theology of land, agriculture rises through sweat into a sacred guardianship of the soil that contains the complete circle of our lives, our source and our destination.

Many cultures have, in awe and gratitude, blessed the mysteries of the earth. Their gods arose from the natural world. But Christianity has looked beyond the earth for blessing: Heaven, not dust, has been the ultimate goal. In Christianity and in Judaism, union with a transcendent God, not communion with nature, is what gives life spiritual meaning. Just as a fish is not aware of the water that carries it, we have taken the soil—the literal ground of our being—for granted, even as it slips away.

Historian Lynn White has drawn a direct connection between this otherworldly theology and our ecologic crisis. He argues that by separating God from nature and putting mankind in charge of a profane world, the Judeo-Christian tradition created a spiritual imbalance that set the stage for the industrial revolution and its attendant abuse of the environment.[1] He perceives the basic tenets of this theology as follows:

- God, as Creator, is separate from and transcendent over nature.
- Made in the image of God, human beings also transcend nature.
- Nature is dead matter and, as such, is profane.
- Human beings, who have been given dominion over nature by God, may use it as they choose for their own purposes.
- Christianity's linear conception of time—as beginning with Genesis and ending with Armageddon—has led to the idea that human culture should continually strive to escape the cycles of nature.

Although all cultures have abused the earth, White believes that pre-Christian ideas of animism and pantheism, which found divinity inherent in nature, counterbalanced humankind's natural tendency to exploit the environment. He argues that the slow deforestation and erosion that occurred throughout history, even in neolithic times, were in no way comparable to modern devastation. It was the Christian conception of mankind as the center of the cosmos, he believes, that produced a change so fundamental that it destroyed all restraint.[2]

It was a long way from Eden and Galilee to the modern industrial state. The path from our basic assertions about the nature of matter and spirit wound endlessly through Greek influences on Christianity, through Renaissance humanism and the Enlightenment, before ever it arrived at the scientific worldview.

Medieval people viewed the cosmos and human society as one harmonious organism, ordered and hierarchical. But implicit within medieval Christian thought was a profound revulsion against the corruptions of the flesh. Perhaps this reflected the influence of Platonic idealism, which held that the "real" world is not the world of the senses, of pain and change and death, but an ideal realm of incorruptible archetypes. Against the earthiness of medieval village life stand the piety, chastity, and obedience, the voluntary poverty and asceticism of the monastery.

Renaissance humanism must have seemed like a fresh wind after the stagnation of divinely imposed order and limit. In the thinking of Francis Bacon, knowledge became power. And this power was human power—on earth, not in a heaven of ideas. The mind became the instrument for asserting human mastery over the world. Modern science was born. René Descartes posited a science devoid of emotion and values, one that reduced all the world to mathematical constructs. John Locke proposed material self-interest as humankind's primary value. And Adam Smith went so far as to define the common good as the accumulation of individual self-interest. Darwin completed this abandonment of spiritual values by describing the foundation of life itself as function and opportunism.

It was thus, in the eyes of Jeremy Rifkin, that the world moved from the sacred to the secular. The meaning of human life was no longer seen in terms of a relationship with the divine, but in the "efficiency, utility, expediency, instrumentality" of a science based on power over nature. Human beings and the universe itself came to be viewed as machines.[3]

This rationalistic conception of the world was probably a necessary precursor of the technosphere that now enmeshes the earth in a microwave communications network, the "nervous system" of a great mechanical contrivance. It seems likely, even, that by providing a blueprint this early visualization created our present reality. Or perhaps an even earlier vision of human power has been projected onto the world. In chapter 3 it was suggested that the Faust tale might help us to understand ourselves. We ask again, could it be that we, like Faust, have been "caught in the devil's bargain," selling our souls for knowledge and power in this world? Have we "materialized" our need for spiritual growth by translating it into a desire for increased wealth? Have we confused our need to connect with nature with a desire to possess and manipulate resources and land? Whether or not this is true, Lynn White believes that until humankind accepts the right of nature to exist in and for itself, things will only get worse. And our historic unwillingness to do this—whether it arises from the root of our religion or is a later growth that twists its branches into burls—is essentially a spiritual problem.

"Since the roots of our ecologic crisis are so largely religious," White concludes, "the remedy must also be essentially religious, whether we call it that or not. We must rethink and refeel our nature and destiny."[4]

White's arguments have stirred response within theological and academic communities. Lewis W. Moncrief seems to excuse humankind for an ignorance that sees in nature's abundance an obstacle to human purposes. He believes the egocentric tendencies of human beings cannot be eliminated by culture.[5] René Dubos argues that we have always and everywhere "pillaged nature" in the pursuit of our immediate advantage. Sound land management techniques are, to him, more essential to a sustainable agriculture than are belief systems. He notes that Japan and Western Europe, with very different philosophies, have maintained their land for thousands of years. Retreating from the Judeo-Christian tradition would be no solution. He calls instead for a new definition of progress based on a more complete understanding of nature and of each ecosystem's particular limitations and potentialities.[6]

Whether a belief system—a worldview, a conception of self and place in nature—really affects behavior is a perennial question. Most people think beliefs form the context in which we operate. In chapter seven we discussed Joseph Campbell's idea that belief systems are the energy-releasing devices for human culture.[7] Myths, religions, ethical systems lend power to our work in the world. They are something to live and die for. The covenant establishing the Jewish nation as God's people, for example, has for centuries sustained Jews, just as the related concept of the promised land motivated American Pilgrims to carve the "City of God" out of wilderness. In like manner, the Judeo-Christian ideal of stewardship could, if taken seriously, become a major tool for releasing the human energy necessary to reverse the growing momentum toward ecological disaster.

Obviously, not everyone believes in the power of myth, and we are constantly offered technological, legal, and political fixes for the problems that plague modern life. Chemicals, computers, genetic or social engineering, shock therapy, and automation are just a few treatments a technological society proposes for its ills. On the land, too, more technology is all too often the solution suggested for problems created by technology.

But what if our problems are *spiritual*? What if the "bottom line" and efficiency have forced us to sacrifice what is most important to us? What if we need to reconnect ethics and spirituality to technology, the economy, the land? What if the whole underlying mythos has been wrong?

Beginning with "Strangers and Guests," a pastoral letter from the Heartland Bishops of the Catholic Church, and the American Lutheran Church's statement "The Land," theologians from almost all American churches have considered these questions. They have published statements and books that derive a land ethic from Old and New Testament principles of love, justice, and service. Turning away from the detachment of science, they have affirmed the centrality of spiritual values. They have reexamined traditional religious assumptions about what we are and how we fit into the scheme of things. They have brought neglected ideas into the light. Theologians, Jewish and Christian, have moved to reestablish religious value restraints upon our dealings with the natural world, reasserting the ancient ideal of stewardship.

Judaism

Jewish scholars are searching in the basic Scriptures of the Torah and the rabbinical teachings of the Talmud for environmental rules. And they are finding them. They have now begun to describe Judaism as an environmental religion, on the basis of teachings long submerged or misunderstood. David Ehrenfeld and Philip Bentley assert that "The chasm between humanity and the rest of nature exists more for Christians than for Jews," who consider earth and spirit to be "part of a greater inseparable whole."[8] Judaism, says Richard H. Schwartz, asserts that "There is one God who created the entire earth as a unity, in ecological balance, and that everything is connected to everything else." A Talmudic story he cites implies that people don't own the land; the land owns people.[9]

Judaism, nevertheless, has historically seen the earth as a resource, implying that although the earth belongs to God, every living thing has a human use. Human beings find salvation in obedience to commandments to be careful stewards, accountable to God, say Ehrenfeld and Bentley. In contrast, Jainism, one of the religions of India, asserts that all things in nature have a right to exist free of human reference, that absolute noninterference and nonviolence are the human role.[10]

Both are extreme views. Human beings, in order to exist, will always interfere to some extent with the rest of nature and had best act with humility and restraint. But even stewardship is easily corrupted by arrogance. How can we know when we are truly operating with the well-being of the land in mind? How can we resist the temptation to play God? Scholars find that the Torah and the Talmud abound with admonishments.

The foundation of Jewish environmental law is the proclamation "The Earth is the Lord's and the fullness thereof." Human beings are no more than "strangers and sojourners" in it. Each command, or *mitzvah,* is supposed to make us creative, not destructive, humbly recognizing our dependence upon God and nature, says Schwartz. Only if we recognize our obligation as stewards can we lay claim to the earth.[11] Such expectations of "accountability and submission," notes Old Testament scholar Walter Brueggemann, "preclude every imagined autonomy."[12]

Nevertheless, commentators have looked to Genesis for the roots of our ecological crisis. But Genesis provides *two* visions of mankind's role on earth. In Genesis 1:26, according to one commentary, *kabash* ("subdue") was used to mean to tread down, bring into bondage (in some accounts, to rape); *radah* ("rule") meant to trample or prevail against. In Genesis 2:15, *abad* ("till, keep") meant till, keep, serve, be a slave to; *shamar* ("take care of") meant keep, watch, preserve.[13] Jewish scholars assert that there is no evidence these verbs were ever interpreted as a license for environmental exploitation. Such exploitation is contrary to the spirit and teaching of the oral law, according to Ehrenfeld and Bentley. They further say English translations of the original Hebrew often prove inadequate because "the difference of structure and word content between the two languages is too great."

According to tenth-century Rabbi Solomon Isaac, they note, one Hebrew word for dominion, *yirdu,* connotes both "dominion" (derived from *radah*) and "descent" (derived from *yarad*). The rabbi understood this to mean, "When man is worthy, he has dominion over the animal kingdom; when he is not, he descends below their level and the animals rule over him."[14]

The research of theologian Robert Gordis suggests that the idea of dominion (or subduing the earth) was related to God's command to man to "be fruitful and multiply," and that the use of a harsh and military verb indicated that this was a male responsibility.[15] Despite past misinterpretations, all now call for stewardship and a dominion based on restraint, humility, and a sense of the sacredness of creation.

Land is a central image to both Judaism and Christianity. The Bible abounds with agricultural references and parables. At the time, that was the way of life. And the promised land has come to mean a time of harmony and peace, a time of *shalom.* Within the Talmud, the laws governing the settling of land, *yishuv ha-aretz* and *yishuv ha-olam,* were intended to guide human behavior so as to create and maintain a properly balanced, sustainable human environment, we are told. They suggest an awareness of the material world and an understanding that salvation is worked out in one's daily choices to do well or ill.

Many of Judaism's environmental laws are based on the principle of *bal tashlit,* which means "do not destroy." Originally this was a ban against destroying an enemy's trees during war, but it has been expanded over time to prohibit other destruction of the environment—and even of human possessions—because all things belong, ultimately, to God. Pollution, waste and overconsumption are also seen as forms of destruction thereby prohibited. Equated with idol worship, violation was officially, though perhaps not actually, punishable by banishment from the community.

The ban on destruction is also expressed in the terms of the observance of the Sabbath. On the Sabbath, Jews are to recognize God's supremacy as Creator by creating nothing themselves. They are to reemphasize God's ownership of the world by destroying nothing. By simply enjoying the bounty of the earth, they are to remind themselves that God, not their own work, is the ultimate source of all good things.[16]

Judaism also declared a Sabbath for the land, the sabbatical, which reasserted God's ultimate dominion over earth. Every seven years the land was to lie fallow to recover its fertility. Because the land was God's, says Gordis, the poor were entitled to whatever grew on it during this time.[17] During the sabbatical, we are told, farmers were to rest, learn, and restore their spiritual values.

The vision of human society presented by the Torah contradicts the economic values that govern technical and industrial civilization. It defines humankind as God's partner in protecting the earth. Stewardship provides the foundation of its economic system. Our more strictly economic values, on the other hand, would have us use the earth's resources for maximum profit without regard for environmental health or future generations. Unmindful of *bal tashlit,* we buy, use, and discard in an "orgy of consumption" and planned obsolescence. The volume and toxicity of our waste endanger the world. The Torah declares a sabbatical for the earth, but our agricultural system strives to produce more and more, devouring fossil fuels, water, and soil, even to the point of putting itself out of business.[18]

The environmental rules of the Torah were originally meant not to protect the environment, but to define a moral life. Care of the world was part of the rabbinic image of a good person. But now, as we begin to look beyond ourselves, to really see the world and our responsibility for its welfare, we can find valid environmental laws in these ancient principles. Perhaps finding these justifications for a change of heart within our religious tradition will help release the energy necessary for change.

Christianity

Christianity rose out of Judaism and shares its Scriptures, basic values, and the dilemma of the concept of dominion. Much of the same scriptural evidence has recently been used to redefine Christianity's theology of land. Christian theologians do not deny their religion's alienation from the creation. And perhaps because they are so troubled by the split between spirit and matter, they have gone a long way to try to heal it.

Though the story of the Fall is common to both religions, it plays a far more pivotal role in Christianity than in Judaism. Christians view the Fall as the original sin that makes redemption necessary for humankind *and* the natural world. For Christians, the Fall upset the natural order of creation, separating us from God. All further schisms, be they within human beings, between human beings, between humankind and nature, or within nature (including, of course, environmental and social problems), result from this basic alienation caused by human sin.[19]

Neither animal nor angel, humankind has been caught in the crease: at times rejecting flesh, at times spirit, but rarely holding it all together. Christians have consistently viewed their natural aspects as a threat to salvation: creature comforts—"the world, the flesh, and the devil"—seduce the soul from the life of the spirit. Reminded constantly to be "in the world but not of it" until Armageddon ends all evil and disharmony, Christians have tended to see this world as a temporary place of preparation for Eternity.

Some theologians argue that it is not the essence of Christianity to devalue the natural world. Pre-Christian ideas have been accepted by Christendom as gospel, and it is a "sign of our fallenness," they say, that we do not heed the commands of the Scriptures to keep the earth. Instead, seeing the body as the prison of the soul and nature as flawed and impermanent, Christians have expressed a Platonistic contempt for God's manifest creation. For such believers, the only true reality exists on a spiritual plane, and the earth is merely the backdrop for the morality play of humankind's salvation.[20] Historically, Christians have been waiting for Christ to come again to save them out of nature.

Others believe the problem lies in Christendom's application of the gospel. Through the ages, pietistic tendencies have militated against the burdens of stewardship. Christians have too often confined their faith to strictly a personal relationship with God, directing good works to those within their communities, but seeing no link between religion and politics and economics. This tendency is seen to be part of a general "desanctification of creation" that denigrates material realities, including the land.

The biblical command to feed the hungry, clothe the naked, and care for the sick has been focused on the realm of the spirit, leaving physical needs neglected.[21] Similarly, the promised land is not the land we till and keep day by day. Even the concept of stewardship has been degraded from caring for God's world to donating a portion of one's wealth to the work of the church.

But scholars are finding scriptural evidence to bring Christianity back down to earth. William M. Swartley says that *Adam,* the Hebrew word for mankind, was described in Genesis 2:7 as created from the ground *(adamah).* This connection of mankind and ground continues throughout Genesis: "When man (Adam) sinned, the *ground* (adamah) was cursed and man's own curse included his struggle against the thorns and thistles of the *ground* and eventual return to *ground,* for out of it mankind was made."[22] A recently published Lutheran land ethic points out that the word *dam,* or lifeblood, is the root of both *Adam* and *adamah.*[23] The lifeblood flowing through mankind also flows through the ground and all of creation. Dust to dust.

Indeed, in our day of ecological crisis, it is easy to see a correspondence between our spiritual state and the condition of the land. Our failure to accept the responsibilities of stewardship, or even to understand that our lives arise out of the soil, is making deserts of fertile ground. This failure poisons rivers, groundwater, and the very rain that falls. In the logic of the prophets Isaiah, Jeremiah, and Micah, the welfare of the ecosphere depends upon the morality and spirituality of the people. When the people fall away, says Swartley, the land mourns, becoming barren.[24] Damaged land is a record of our ancient myths of alienation from it. But though our separateness is but a myth, its consequences are real. As poet Meridel LeSueur has written:

> Nature returns all wounds as warriors.
> The Earth plans resistance and cries, "Live."[25]

Considering the external world of commerce, science, technology, politics, and social life to be the "real world," Western civilization has been markedly extroverted. Even with its ideal of the saint dedicated to action, Christianity has "render[ed] unto Caesar the things which are Caesar's and unto God the things which are God's." One of the things thereby rendered to

God is the introverted life of the spirit. "Even the (individualistic and nonworldly) disciplines of the Christian life—prayer, Bible-study, meditation, and worship—center around a private religion," observes a stewardship study. But, perhaps because of the seriousness of our environmental situation, it continues, thinkers within the churches now say we must attempt to "heal and restore the relationship between God and *all* His creation by these disciplines."[26] And not only by these disciplines, but by envisioning a new theology of land.

Traditionally, Western peoples have considered nature—including animals, plants, and the land itself—as property to be bought, sold, inherited, exploited. Its value exists in its use for mankind. In order to sue to protect a resource in a court of law, one has to demonstrate that one's use of that resource is impaired by someone else's actions.[27] The fact that we call trees, minerals, water, and soil *resources* shows how we regard them. On its roadsigns, the state of New Mexico even proclaims itself a "land of many uses." Christians are now beginning to see the world as having value in and for itself apart from any human use. "Nothing in the universe," they say, "is mere raw material" to be consumed for our happiness.[28]

Historically, Christians have kept God separate from nature. Humankind is seen to be the intelligence and consciousness of a nature created out of nothing, as a free act of will,[29] by a transcendent and independent God who has a divine purpose for the world.[30] Though nature is recognized by God to be good, and exists in part to give God glory,[31] nature is not by this view divine, having instead a "derived dignity" as a good creation of the Giver. Worship of land is considered idolatrous.[32]

For some Christian thinkers, God is no longer independent of creation. This is not, however, according to Wes Granberg-Michaelson, tantamount to pantheism. A more scriptural, though untraditional, concept he introduces is the idea that "the creation flowed forth (or emanated) naturally from the life of the Creator . . . God, rather than nothingness, is the source of creation" and cannot be separate from it.[33]

Within Christianity, Christ is the incarnation of God in human flesh (*incarnation* means "into flesh"). As true God and yet true man, Christ is a mediator between earth and heaven who conquered death and ascended *bodily* into heaven to return at the end of time to redeem creation and resurrect the *bodies* of the faithful. Though others have declared the sacrament of communion a symbolic one, some major denominations believe they become one with Christ by partaking of his *body* and *blood,* which are mystically present in the earthly bread and wine. These ideas, in themselves, suggest a belief that spirit and flesh, like matter and energy, constantly convert one into the other. But theologians have also gone back to the old idea that Christ is *within* creation as the *logos,* present from the beginning. John 1:3–4 says, "All things were made through him, and without him was not anything made that was made. In him was life, and the life was the light of men." The idea of Christ as the Word, the divine *logos,* the informing, sustaining, ordering principle of the cosmos, born into the flesh of this world

> revises somewhat . . . the Christian doctrine of transcendence with a doctrine of immanence. Though God, the Creator, is indeed beyond the world, He is also in it. The historical Incarnation is the center, the exemplification in time, of God's willingness in Christ to create, sustain, delight in, and (if necessary) sacrificially *redeem* creation.[34]

If what holds the universe in its way is divine, we have only imagined a split between nature and spirit. Carry this idea to its logical conclusion and the universe becomes one divine body of which we are a part, our every act a sacrament of communion with it.

In the new theology, Christ is not only immanent, but a model for human stewardship. As true God, Christ has dominion over the cosmos, which he exercises by becoming a servant. Christians are to become for nature what Christ became for them. As "joint-heirs with Christ," Christians would assume a new responsibility.[35] Christ's virtues of compassion, trustworthiness, humility, and self-sacrifice[36] would inspire Christians to sacrifice in order to bring harmony to the world.[37]

Stewardship is a sort of trusteeship that holds humankind accountable for creation. The idea of Christ as model steward adds love and self-sacrifice and redemption, but does nothing to change the inherent inequality between humankind and nature. Dominion, even if tempered by love, is a relationship implying power over another, and as such contains the possibility of arrogance.

The Christian tradition, however, has for centuries also encompassed the Franciscan idea of humankind's equality with nature. In his "Canticle of Brother Sun, Sister Moon," Saint Francis praised the elements of nature as glorious expressions of God, calling wind, water, fire, and the earth "brother" and "sister." Francis is typically pictured in a garden, exorting the birds to praise God as they alight on his hands. Animals gather at his feet in peace. Similarly, the Native American describes natural objects as his relatives. Dominion is excluded and action is limited by such relatedness. Fear and competition have, for centuries, made these ideas the province of visionaries, but now that nature has been, for the moment, essentially "mastered," perhaps more of us will feel we can afford to affirm our relatedness to it. Saint Francis, "the greatest spiritual revolutionary in Western history," may yet become, as Lynn White suggests, the patron saint of ecologists.[38]

Theologian Elizabeth Dodson Gray proposes a relatedness to the natural world that is one of kinship. She sees all members of the natural world as equal. But human beings, from within nature, make decisions that affect the welfare of other equal members. We must, therefore, "appreciate diversity and reward it—without ranking it." We should learn to find "value in each part as well as in the welfare of the whole," just as parents make decisions about what will benefit each individual child and the family as a unit. In such a relationship, she says, "all species would be validated by their basic imprimatur of worth given to them in the creation itself."[39]

For eons humankind has been the prodigal child of Mother Nature, demanding that she feed and clothe us for nothing, bear away our wastes, and endlessly forgive our sins against her. We have seldom acted in good faith or expressed maturity in this relationship. Can we now celebrate the "family" ties that bind us to the earth, the life force that flows through all? Can we return home to heal and "mother" Mother Earth, just as a grown child cares for a sick and aging parent? It may be that nothing less will assure our survival.

Redemption

Can we come home again? Can we reconfigure our theology so to enable us to relax into being what we are? Elizabeth Dodson Gray questions the whole notion of our alienation from the earth: "What if the Fall was not down into sin and our worst self but more ironically a Fall *up* in which we fail to accept or 'claim' our full humanness, and the finitude of our bodies, and our mortality, and our trajectory toward dying? What if our Fall was *up* into the illusion that we were above dying, above mortality, above and apart from creation?"[40]

To a large degree theologians have given up this illusion. They now say that we are so totally integrated into the processes of nature that salvation can no longer be an otherworldly concern. As Loren Wilkinson observes: "We simply cannot escape our embeddedness in nature or nature's embeddedness in us. Therefore, our knowledge seems to indicate that we can no longer speak of being saved out of nature; we are redeemed *in* nature, not apart from it. In the same way the Christian must include the rest of creation in his or her salvation."[41]

Most religious systems, according to Joseph Campbell, seek to bring human beings into accord with nature. But in the Western tradition, when Adam and Eve succumbed to the lure of knowledge, all of nature fell with them. The problem for Christianity has not been to get into accord with nature, but to attempt to correct it. Rejecting the idea that human beings are only souls temporarily cursed with robes of flesh leaves us with the problem of explaining evil in the world. Flesh and blood beings, inseparable from the matrix out of which we arose, need redemption. And matter must be corrected, that is to say, redeemed along with us.

Why do we feel that nature needs redeeming? It would seem that this attitude reveals a continuing alienation. But what we call things—what they represent for us and how we relate to them—does make a difference. If we must "redeem" nature in order to save it, so be it. Perhaps such talk is only another way of saying nature is holy.

Theologians now ask whether it is "an indication of our fallen condition that we humans, all too often, have interpreted the sacrificial death of Christ as being *only* for our own personal salvation," when the Scriptures clearly state that "Jesus came to save the world *(cosmos)*, not just humankind."[42] Isaiah's Old Testament vision of the Messiah contributes to this view by speaking of a total restoration of the whole of creation at the end of time.[43]

Wilkinson has turned to Eastern Orthodox Christianity's belief in the "goodness of matter, its redeemability and its dependence upon humans for its access to that divine redemption."[44] And Wes Granberg-Michaelson understands redemption as the fulfillment of God's intention for the world: the completion of the covenant that God made not only with humankind but with "every living creature that is with you, the birds, the cattle, and every beast of the earth," in the words of Genesis 8 and 9. Granberg-Michaelson sees the fulfillment of this covenant, as presented in Hosea 2:18–23, to be a vision in which humanity, nature, and God are wedded:

> Then I will make a covenant on behalf of Israel with the wild beasts, the birds of the air, and things that creep on the earth, and I will break bow and sword and weapon of war and sweep them off the earth, so that all living creatures may lie down without fear. I will betroth you to myself forever, betroth you in lawful wedlock with unfailing devotion and love; I will betroth you to myself to have and to hold, and you shall know the Lord.[45]

This betrothal, this union of humankind, nature, and God in harmony and peace—*shalom*—is a return to the garden. It is the messianic age that Israel has so long awaited; it is the millennium of Christianity's hope. Walter Brueggemann says, "The ultimate promise of the Old Testament is that blessed communion with God is in the land—whatever that metaphor means." He believes that "unless we reinterpret the Bible in terms of materiality and Jewish bodily reality . . . we will go on in our society being hopelessly alienated. Land theology is rooted in a discussion of what makes for death and what makes for abundant life. And that requires us to understand that materiality is what our creatureliness is all about."[46]

In *Judaism and Global Survival,* Richard H. Schwartz applies Jewish values to an activist redemption of the earth. He believes that the values of the Torah can help solve our environmental crisis. "As co-workers with God," he says, "charged with the task of being a light unto the nations and of *tikun olam* (restoring and redeeming the earth), it is essential that Jews . . . work with others for radical changes in our economic and production systems, our values, and our life-styles, based on the important biblical mandate to work with God in preserving the earth."[47] Jewish theologians point out that creation is an ongoing process, renewed daily, and that we must appreciate the everyday workings of nature, for "there is no miracle greater than the continued existence of the natural order."[48]

Christian theologian C. Dean Freudenberger thinks "time is running out." He says the church must first understand the problem, and then understand that the ecological crisis on our farms is caused by human alienation from creation. If nurture is constantly shaped by religious understanding of our being in the image of God, he says, then ecological farming is possible. It is the task of the church to lay judgment upon what is wrong and advocate work on that which can still be regenerated.[49]

Christianity echoes Hosea's picture of betrothal with a vision that heals the split between matter and spirit, cancelling the curse of "dust to dust" in divine communion. Contemporary Eastern Orthodox theologian Alexander Schmemann uses the Christian symbology of the Eucharist to describe what he believes to be the creative role for humans in this world:

> The first, the basic definition of man is that he is the *priest*. He stands in the center of the world and unifies it in his act of blessing God, of both receiving the world from God and offering it to God—and by filling the world with this eucharist, he transforms his life, the one that he receives from the world, into life in God, into communion with Him. The world was created as the "matter," the material of one all-embracing eucharist, and man was created as the priest of this cosmic sacrament.[50]

In 1949, when conservationist Aldo Leopold called for an extension of the field of ethics, he proposed that we include not only all people within our ethical framework, but also the land. "A land ethic," he said, "changes the role of Homo sapiens from conqueror of the land-community to plain member and citizen of it."[51] Theologians seem to have answered Leopold's call. They have reexamined Judaic and Christian teachings and are beginning to form a scripturally based land ethic that reinterprets "dominion" as participation in the ongoing process of creation. They have been "re-thinking and re-feeling our nature and destiny," as Lynn White suggested they do, and in the process, have reimposed religious value-restraints on our use of land and resources. To the degree that they succeed, it will no longer be possible for spiritually conscious Jews or Christians to freely abuse or exploit the environment.

As we have seen, the Jewish and Christian traditions already contain the concepts needed to inspire true stewardship of the earth. It is extremely significant that so many major American religious groups have agreed in both their analysis and their conclusions on matters of land stewardship. Soon we will see whether religious ideas and ideals really do influence action.

It is as if the entire history of the Judeo-Christian tradition has been contained within the thrust, lift-off, and trajectory of a rocketship bent upon leaving the earth, escaping the curse of "dust to dust." Perhaps such detachment was necessary for the establishment of systems that have freed us from dulling bondage to the struggle for survival. Perhaps a judicious application of technology could, like the sabbatical, sufficiently free us from "getting and spending" to allow us to pursue spiritual goals. But our technology has to this point freed very few from struggle and has, itself, become a threat to the survival of our planet. We must change our relationship, not only to technology, but to nature. We must accept the earth as it is, obey its laws, surrender to time and change and cycle. With the God of Genesis we must say on each new day, "This is good."

Could it be that we needed to almost lose the world in order to find it? Did we need alienation in order to realize our need for communion? Within the new theology, humankind comes all the way around to a *conscious* stewardship based on true compassion and awareness. Dominion becomes service; competition is tempered by cooperation. The lion and the lamb within us lie down together. And in full knowledge of our inseparability from the land, we learn to nurture and sustain it for all foreseeable time as the source of our life and our only home.

Joseph Campbell tells us that "in our tradition the holy land is somewhere else"; it is not the land under our feet that sustains us. As Americans, we are a nation of newcomers, with roots in every land but our own. In 1933, Chief Luther Standing Bear wrote: "The man from Europe is still a foreigner and an alien . . . But in the Indian the spirit of the land is still vested; it will be until other men are able to divine and meet its rhythms.

Men must be born and reborn to belong. Their bodies must be formed of the dust of their forefather's bones."[52] Perhaps now, fifty years later, we can stop thinking of ourselves as "strangers and sojourners in it." Perhaps after generations of inhabiting this continent, the dust of our forefathers has begun to enter our bones and the spirit of this land our theology. After more than 200 years of waste and destruction, perhaps we are beginning to divine and meet its rhythms, to find in our traditions the words that will call this land, and indeed all the earth, holy land.

NOTES

All biblical quotations unless part of a reference to another source are from the *Revised Standard Version* (New York: Thomas Nelson & Sons, 1953).

1. Lynn White, Jr., "The Historical Roots of Our Ecologic Crisis," in David and Eileen Spring, eds., *Ecology and Religion in History* (New York: Harper Torchbooks, Harper & Row, 1974), pp. 24–25.
2. Ibid., pp. 16–18.
3. Jeremy Rifkin, in Philip Zaleski and Peggy Taylor, "Conversations with a Heretic," *New Age Journal*, November 1985, p. 45.
4. White, Jr., pp. 30–31.
5. Lewis W. Moncrief, "The Cultural Basis for Our Environmental Crisis," in *Ecology and Religion in History*, pp. 76–90.
6. René Dubos, "Franciscan Conservation vs. Benedictine Stewardship," in *Ecology and Religion in History*, pp. 114–46.
7. See Joseph Campbell, *The Masks of God: Primitive Mythology* (New York: Viking, 1959), p. 4.
8. David Ehrenfeld and Philip J. Bentley, "Stewardship Started with the Jews," *Plow-Share*, 1 Winter 1984, pp. 13–17.
9. Richard H. Schwartz, *Judaism and Global Survival* (New York: Vantage Press, 1984), pp. 45–47.
10. Ehrenfeld and Bentley, pp. 12, 18.
11. Schwartz, pp. 45, 47.
12. Walter Brueggemann, "Theses on Land in the Bible," in *Erets: Land* (Amesville, OH: Coalition for Appalachian Ministry, n.d.).
13. James R. Hinkley, *Stewardship of the Land in North Carolina*, The Land Stewardship Council of North Carolina, Inc. (Raleigh, NC: 1982), p. 15.
14. Ehrenfeld and Bentley, pp. 12–13.
15. Robert Gordis, "Ecology in the Jewish Tradition," *Midstream*, October 1985, p. 19.
16. Ehrenfeld and Bentley, pp. 6, 12, 14.
17. Gordis, p. 22.
18. Schwartz, pp. 50–51.
19. Hinkley, p. 7.

20. Loren Wilkinson et al., eds., *Earthkeeping: Christian Stewardship of Natural Resources* (Grand Rapids, MI: Wm. B. Eerdmans Publishing Co., 1980), pp. 105–6.
21. Hinkley, p. 24.
22. William M. Swartley, "Biblical Sources of Stewardship," in Mary Evelyn Jegen and Bruno V. Manno, eds., *The Earth Is the Lord's: Essays on Stewardship* (New York: Paulist Press, 1978), p. 25.
23. *The Land* (Minneapolis: Augsburg Publishing House, 1982).
24. Swartley, p. 36.
25. Meridel LeSueur, "Dòan Kêt," in *Rites of Ancient Ripening* (Minneapolis: Vanilla Press, 1975), p. 52.
26. Hinkley, p. 9.
27. Christopher D. Stone, *Should Trees Have Standing: Toward Legal Rights for Natural Objects* (New York: Avon Books, 1975), pp. 31–32.
28. Wilkinson, p. 260.
29. Wes Granberg-Michaelson, "Earthkeeping: A Theology for Global Sanctification," *Sojourners,* October 1982, p. 22.
30. Wilkinson, p. 258.
31. Ibid., p. 205.
32. *The Land,* p. 3.
33. Granberg-Michaelson, p. 22.
34. Wilkinson, p. 217.
35. Ibid., p. 218.
36. William J. Byron, "The Ethics of Stewardship," in *The Earth Is the Lord's,* p. 45.
37. Hinkley, p. 16.
38. White, Jr., pp. 29, 30–31.
39. Elizabeth Dodson Gray, *Green Paradise Lost* (Wellesley, MA: Roundtable Press, 1979), pp. 148–49.
40. Ibid., p. 158.
41. Wilkinson, p. 4.
42. Hinkley, p. 9.
43. *The Land,* p. 3.
44. Wilkinson, p. 222.
45. Granberg-Michaelson, p. 23.
46. Brueggemann, p. 9.
47. Schwartz, p. 52.
48. Ehrenfeld and Bentley, p. 14.
49. C. Dean Freudenberger, speech at Ostmark Lutheran Church, Meeker County, MN, October 1985.
50. Wilkinson, p. 222.
51. Aldo Leopold, *A Sand County Almanac with Essays on Conservation from Round River* (New York: Ballantine Books, 1970), p. 239.
52. Chief Luther Standing Bear, in T. C. McLuhan, ed., *Touch the Earth* (New York: Pocket Books, 1972), p. 107.

· 9 ·

Native American Stewardship

> The original instructions of the Creator are universal and valid for all time. The essence of these instructions is compassion for all life and love for all creation. We must realize that we do not live in a world of dead matter, but in a universe of living spirit. Let us open our eyes to the sacredness of Mother Earth, or our eyes will be opened for us.[1]
>
> Grandfather David Monongye

THESE words of a Hopi grandfather spring from a basic attitude of reverence for the world shared by most Native Americans, past and present. T. C. McLuhan, in her anthology of Indian statements about nature, *Touch the Earth,* writes: "When Black Elk . . . speaks of the 'beauty and strangeness of the earth,' he speaks of reverence for the everyday environment that was integrally interwoven with Indian life. . . . Who the Indians were could not without serious loss be separated from where and how they lived."[2] Though we live in a technological age that modifies the environment at every turn, we would do well to look closely at the religion that allowed the original Americans to live in harmony with the land. Undoubtedly, we will not return to their pretechnological life-style, but it may be that the ideals of "compassion for all life and love for all creation" could help us to adapt our technological society to natural processes, thus making it as sustainable and renewable as those processes themselves.

Relationship to Nature

For Native Americans, the earth was Mother and the sky was Father. The circle expressed for them the idea that all things were in harmony. In this selection from his biography, Black Elk, an Oglala Sioux holy man, sees circles everywhere:

> You have noticed that everything an Indian does is in a circle, and that is because the Power of the World always works in circles, and everything tries to be round. In the old days, when we were a strong and happy people, all our power came to us from the sacred hoop of the nation and so long as the hoop was unbroken the people flourished. The flowering tree was the living center of the hoop, and the circle of the four quarters nourished it. The east gave peace and light, the south gave warmth, the west gave rain, and the north with its cold and mighty wind gave strength and endurance. This knowledge came to us from the outer world with our religion. Everything the Power of the World does is done in a circle. The sky is round and I have heard that the Earth is round like a ball and so are all the stars. The Wind, in its greatest power, whirls. Birds make their nests in circles, for theirs is the same religion as ours. The sun comes forth and goes down again in a circle. The moon does the same, and both are round.
>
> Even the seasons form a great circle in their changing, and always come back again to where they were. The life of a man is a circle from childhood to childhood and so it is in everything where power moves. Our tipis were round like the nests of birds and these were always set in a circle, the nation's hoop, a nest of many nests, where the Great Spirit meant for us to hatch our children.[3]

In this poem from a Pawnee ceremony, the mothering power of nature that day by day sustains life is seen to be miraculous, not taken for granted.

THE BIRTH OF DAWN, FROM THE HAKO

Earth our mother, breathe forth life
all night sleeping
now awaking
in the east
now see the dawn

Earth our mother, breathe and waken
leaves are stirring
all things moving
new day coming
life renewing

Eagle soaring, see the morning
see the new mysterious morning
something marvelous and sacred
though it happens every day
Dawn the child of God and Darkness[4]

From the Blue Lake, high in the mountains of north-central New Mexico, a little river flows down through the Taos Pueblo. In all the 900-year history of that arid settlement, the river has never gone dry. These recorded words of a Taos Indian show an identification with this lake and all other elements of the nature which sustains that community:

Blue lake of life from which flows everything good,
We rejoice with the spirits beneath your waters.
The lake and the earth and the sky
Are all around us.
The voices of many gods
Are all within us.
We are now as one with rock and tree
As one with eagle and crow
As one with all things
That have been placed here by the Great Spirit.
The sun that shines upon us

The wind that wipes our faces clean of fear
The stars that guide us on this journey
To our blue lake of life
We rejoice with you.
In beauty it is begun.
In beauty it is begun.
In peace it is finished.
In peace it shall never end.[5]

In the following passage, Chief Luther Standing Bear explains the Native American's feeling of relationship to nature, which includes a love of the soil itself as a "mothering power." Connection to the soil heals and gives life; it makes him think and feel and see more clearly his mysterious connection to all life.

> The Lakota was a true naturist—a lover of nature. He loved the earth and all things of the earth, the attachment growing with age. The old people came literally to love the soil and they sat or reclined on the ground with a feeling of being close to a mothering power. It was good for the skin to touch the earth and the old people liked to remove their moccasins and walk with bare feet on the sacred earth. Their tipis were built upon the earth and their altars were made of earth. The birds that flew in the air came to rest upon the earth and it was the final abiding place of all things that lived and grew. The soil was soothing, strengthening, cleansing and healing.
>
> That is why the old Indian still sits upon the earth instead of propping himself up and away from its life-giving forces. For him, to sit or lie upon the ground is to be able to think more deeply and to feel more keenly; he can see more clearly into the mysteries of life and come closer in kinship to other lives about him. . . .
>
> Kinship with all creatures of the earth, sky, and water, was a real and active principle. For the animal and bird world there existed a brotherly feeling that kept the Lakota safe among them and so close did some of the Lakotas come to their feathered and furred friends that in true brotherhood they spoke a common tongue.

> The old Lakota was wise. He knew that man's heart away from nature becomes hard; he knew that lack of respect for growing, living things soon led to lack of respect for humans too. So he kept his youth close to its softening influence.[6]

In her introduction to *Touch the Earth,* T. C. McLuhan characterizes the Indian statements she has compiled: "They speak with courtesy and respect of the land, of animals, of the objects which made up the territory in which they lived. They saw no virtue in imposing their will over their environment: private acquisition, almost without exception, was to them a way to poverty, not to riches. The meaning of their life was identified through their relationships with each other and their homelands."[7]

Throughout *Touch the Earth,* Native Americans speak of their relationship to the Great Spirit, to their own people, to animals and plants, and to the processes and cycles of the natural world. Their words suggest great sensitivity to the mystery and healing power in nature. Nature was treated with awe and was altered only with care and prayerfulness. This statement by a Taos Indian suggests that true necessity should be the guiding principle in our decisions on the use of natural resources:

> The dust is blowing on the mountain. The dust is the mountain growing. The mountain heals itself just like man if you give it time to rest.
>
> Do not move the rock or anything placed in its place by God. Not a leaf from a tree nor a bird from its nest nor a spider's silver thread. These things will fall soon enough in their time.
>
> The earth has roots, and the roots belong to the soil. If you cut a hole in the soil you have damaged the earth. You must therefore be certain it is necessary.[8]

A Wintu woman of California suggests that she actually feels pain when the earth is damaged.

> The White people never cared for the land or deer or bear. When we Indians kill meat, we eat it all up. When we dig roots we make little holes. When we built houses,

> we make little holes. When we burn grass for grasshoppers, we don't ruin things. We shake down acorns and pinenuts. We don't chop down the trees. We only use dead wood. But the White people plow up the ground, pull down the trees, kill everything. The tree says: "Don't. I am sore. Don't hurt me." But they chop it down and cut it up. The spirit of the land hates them. They blast out trees and stir it up to its depths. They saw up the trees. That hurts them. The Indians never hurt anything, but the White people destroy all. They blast rocks and scatter them on the ground. The rock says, "Don't. You are hurting me." But the White people pay no attention. When the Indians use rocks, they take little round ones for their cooking . . . How can the spirit of the earth like the White man? . . . Everywhere the White man has touched, it is sore.[9]

Norman Russell, a modern Native American poet, says he spends much of his time in nature and wants his work to express "respect and . . . enjoyment, this feeling of brotherhood and sisterhood with nature."

> There is a misconception among civilized people that nature is hostile. Nature is not hostile. In nature, the only thing that is hostile to you is something that you're hostile to. . . . It's basically true that you have nothing to fear except your own fear of nature. If you are to trust something, you must understand it and be aware of it and pay close attention to it. For example, when you lie down to sleep out in the middle of the forest somewhere far away from civilization, you will hear a thousand sounds. Then you'll hear a thousand friendly sounds when you get to know them. But if you don't know them, they'll frighten you, the various sounds. In the Great Smokey Mountains, there is a little piney owl, a small white owl, that has this terrible fierce scream. It'll scare you out of your mind, but if you know it's just a little owl out hunting for small mice, why it doesn't frighten you at all. It's a friendly noise. . . .
>
> I really believe in this. It may come from you, but you can feel a comfort alone in the woods and a protection there.[10]

The following Native American poems show a great sensitivity to the "beauty and strangeness of the earth" and a feeling of being part of a vast power beyond human understanding.

THE GREAT SEA

The great sea
Has sent me adrift,
It moves me as the weed in a great river,
Earth and the great weather
Move me,
Have carried me away
And move my inward parts with joy.[11]
Eskimo

IT WAS THE WIND

It was the wind that gave them life. It is the wind that comes out of our mouths now that gives us life. When this ceases to blow we die. In the skin at the tips of our fingers we see the trail of the wind; it shows us where the wind blew when our ancestors were created.[12]

Navajo

An Omaha invocation presents relationship to nature as the central fact of life. Life is a journey on which the individual receives help from the elements, and indeed these elements are asked permission for the beginning of a new human life.

INTRODUCTION OF THE CHILD TO THE COSMOS

Ho! Ye Sun, Moon, Stars, all ye that move in the heavens,
I bid you hear me!
Into your midst has come a new life.
Consent ye, I implore!
Make its path smooth, that it may reach the brow of the first hill!

Ho! Ye Winds, Clouds, Rain, Mist, all ye that move in the air,
I bid you hear me!
Into your midst has come a new life.

Consent ye, I implore!
Make its path smooth, that it may reach the brow of
the second hill!

Ho! Ye Hills, Valleys, Rivers, Lakes, Trees, Grasses,
all ye of the earth,
I bid you hear me!
Into your midst has come a new life.
Consent ye, I implore!
Make its path smooth, that it may reach the brow of
the third hill!

Ho! Ye Birds, great and small, that fly in the air,
Ho! Ye Animals, great and small, that dwell in the
forest,
Ho! Ye Insects that creep among the grasses and
burrow in the ground—
I bid you hear me!
Into your midst has come a new life.
Consent ye, I implore!
Make its path smooth, that it may reach the brow of
the fourth hill!

Ho! All ye of the heavens, all ye of the air, all ye of
the earth;
I bid you all to hear me!
Into your midst has come a new life.
Consent ye, consent ye all, I implore!
Make its path smooth—then shall it travel beyond
the four hills![13]

In this Taos poem, nature is seen as a healing power that melts away human troubles. Those who identify with its elements find peace and strength.

My help is in the mountain
Where I take myself to heal
The earthly wounds
That people give to me.
I find a rock with sun on it
And a stream where the water runs gentle
And the trees which one by one give me company.

So must I stay for a long time
Until I have grown from the rock
And the stream is running through me
And I cannot tell myself from one tall tree.
Then I know that nothing touches me
Nor makes me run away.
My help is in the mountain
That I take away with me.

Earth cure me. Earth receive my woe. Rock strengthen me. Rock receive my weakness. Rain wash my sadness away. Rain receive my doubt. Sun make sweet my song. Sun receive the anger from my heart.[14]

Connectedness to a specific place is also part of the tradition of the Native Americans. The land where their ancestors are buried is sacred to them. They are not merely passive observers of its beauty or recipients of grace, but take responsibility for the harmonious operation of natural processes. To the Taos people, it is humankind's role, through ritual, to sustain that harmony:

One man must always rise
in the dark and go
to the mountain
to greet the sun at dawn.
If man were not to do this
the sun would not rise.[15]

All peoples have attempted to manipulate nature through the use of ritual or technology. All aspects of Native American life, including agriculture, were ritualized. This Hopi Kachina song creates a harmonious picture of healthy, well-watered crops, pollinated by butterflies with the same colors as the blossoms. It creates an image of harmony and correspondence among parts of their world in order to bring this about:

KACHINA SONG

Yellow butterflies for corn blossoms
(with flower-painted maidens' faces)
Blue butterflies over bean blossoms
(with pollen-painted maidens' faces)

Yellow and blue hovering, hovering,
Wild bees singing in and out
Over all black thunder hanging
Over all downpouring rain[16]

This Osage planting song was sung at a girl's initiation to womanhood to show her importance—as planter, cultivator, and harvester of corn—to the life of the group:

PLANTING SONG

I have made a footprint, a sacred one.
I have made a footprint, through it the blades push
upward.
I have made a footprint, through it the blades radiate.
I have made a footprint, over it the blades float in
the wind.
I have made a footprint, over it the ears lean toward
one another.
I have made a footprint, over it the blossoms lie gray.
I have made a footprint, smoke arises from my house.
I have made a footprint, there is cheer in my house.
I have made a footprint, I live in the light of day.[17]

In this poem, a Taos Indian acknowledges his debt to death and life and sees that his eventual death will allow the circle of life to continue.

I have killed the deer.
I have crushed the grasshopper
And the plants he feeds upon.
I have cut through the heart
Of trees growing old and straight.
I have taken fish from water
And birds from the sky.
In my life I have needed death
So that my life can be.
When I dic I must give life
To what has nourished me.
The earth receives my body
And gives it to the plants

And to the caterpillars
To the birds
And to the coyotes
Each in its turn so that
The circle of life is never broken.[18]

Given their relationship to nature, it is not surprising that Native Americans left few scars upon the earth. Europeans turned the concept of the circle into the clocks and wheels of technological power, but Native Americans saw circles in the movements of nature and made a medicine wheel to reflect an inner, spiritual power. It is perhaps this emphasis on inner power that made *relationship* rather than *domination* the focus of Indian life. "All things are contained within the medicine wheel," according to the author of *Seven Arrows,* Hyemeyohst Storm, "and all things are equal within it." And yet humankind has a special place in the wheel. We are determiners.

> All the things of the Universe Wheel have spirit and life, including the rivers, rocks, earth, sky, plants and animals. But it is only man, of all the Beings on the Wheel, who is a determiner. Our determining spirit can be made whole only through the learning of our harmony with all our brothers and sisters, and with all the other spirits of the Universe. To do this we must learn to seek, and to perceive. We must do this to find our place within the Medicine Wheel. To determine this place we must learn to *give-away.*[19]

Certainly humankind has, for the time being, become the "determiner" of what happens in the environment. But we have only rarely found our proper place within the medicine wheel. We have not, as a species, learned to live in harmony with the laws of nature. Instead we have operated mainly from an abstract rational perspective, one that designates the elements of nature as "natural resources" rather than as parts of a matrix for life and living. Storm says we must learn to give away rather than only take from creation. This, of course, is stewardship.

Because our activities constantly interrupt natural processes, we must understand and reconstruct them as we go. By accepting our place as determiner, and learning to give back to the world that sustains us, we find wholeness within ourselves. We are not likely to be plagued by alienation or ennui once we have found our proper role.

Hopi—The Web of the World

There is a curious similarity between the world concepts of modern physics and ecology and the ancient Hopi vision of the universe. They have in common an idea of the universe as an interrelated field, a continuum, a web in which nothing acts independently, everything is part of an inherent harmony.[20] Human beings who are aware of being totally enmeshed in the universe find it hard to tell where they begin and the world leaves off. Their interests are inextricably bound with those of the whole. Obviously, such a view is conducive to good stewardship of the earth because the self comes to include the whole environment.

The entire Hopi cosmology, as Frank Waters describes it, is based upon human connectedness to the universe. The Hopi see their land, the promised land, as the spiritual center of the earth, lying on the magnetic junction of the North-South axis of the poles and the East-West path of the sun.[21] They regard life as a movement along a path to the sun, a process of purification that becomes progressively more difficult. This present world, according to the Hopi tradition, is the fourth world mankind has been given, the other three having been destroyed by greed and disunity, by human lack of respect for God and one another. The first three worlds were simple, but this fourth world is "complete," or complex; all the opposites (positive and negative aspects) are present for humans to choose from.[22]

The Hopi, after an immense odyssey covering most of North America, chose the barrenness of the southwestern United States as their home because in an easier life it would not be necessary to "depend on prayer." They say, "it is only by our faith that our fields are watered. By our prayers the rains come from the clouds."[23] This fourth world, the most grossly materialistic and willful of the four,[24] will also be destroyed if human beings do not adhere to the plan of the Creator.[25]

The Hopi believe in an integral connection between human beings and the earth, and their religion is not separate from everyday life. The sun is both the life-giving physical sun and the spiritual Father. The earth is the Mother, a living entity[26] whose milk is the corn from which the human body is made.[27] Many Hopi rituals take place in a kiva, a square or more often round hole in the earth that is most holy at its deepest part. There are no chosen priests, and all men humbly take part in ceremonies concerned not with individual salvation, but with "cosmic patterns through which all forms of life move to their appointed ends."[28]

The Hopi universe is a harmonious whole wherein all things—plants and animals, human beings, and the vast star systems—exist in a web of interrelated obligations. The task of human beings is to "open the door" so they can merge with this wholeness and come to consciousness of themselves as finite parts of infinity.[29] Every human act must conform to the great universal pattern.[30] Human rituals, the Hopi believe, actually maintain the harmony of the universe, calling down the rain, making the corn grow, turning the sun at the winter solstice "back on its trail to bring ever-lengthening days of light, warmth and life for plants, animals and men."[31] Without this close attention to ritual, the harmony of the world, the world itself, would be endangered.[32]

The Hopi concept of the human being standing at the center of the world, maintaining through every action the harmony of the universe, is an image of good stewardship. The Hopi recognize two great connections in life: all are members of an earthly family and clan as well as "citizens of the great universe" to which they owe "growing allegiance as their understanding develops."[33] As citizens of the universe, the Hopi take responsibility for its harmonious operation. They try, through careful attention to ritual, to create a world in which all things "will sing together in tune with the universal power, in harmony with the one creator of all things. And the bird song and the people's song and the song of life will become one."[34]

Black Elk's Vision

In 1932, a holy man of the Oglala Sioux, Black Elk, told John G. Neihardt of his life and of his great vision. From the "lonely hilltop" of his old age, Black Elk felt his "mighty vision" was "given to a man too weak to use it."[35] He died believing he had been charged with saving his people and that he had failed. But it is not necessary to believe in Black Elk's mission in order to appreciate his vision, one that offers a mythic description of the proper role of each man and woman as a steward of the earth.

At the age of nine, Black Elk was struck down by illness and lifted up into a realm where he "saw more than [he could] tell and . . . understood more than [he] saw."[36] He stood at the "center of the world" while horses of power plunged toward him from the four directions. In Plains Indian cosmology, the center of the world is everywhere. At each point on the surface of the earth the influences of the four directions come together.[37] The North is the white place of cold wisdom, which must be warmed by the life-giving green and feeling realm of the South. The golden East of sunrise and the morning star is the direction of illumination that "sees things clearly far and wide." Its opposite, the West, is the black night—the source of introspection.[38] Surveying the flat, wide-open country of the plains, one is clearly in the center of the great circle of the horizon. This center, where the good red road and the black road of adversity cross each other—the here and now—is seen by the Sioux as sacred. At all times each person walks on one road or the other.

In his vision, Black Elk encounters the grandfathers of the six directions, which include up and down (sky and earth) as well as the four quarters. Each grandfather gives Black Elk a power with which to work in the world. The Grandfather of the West, "where the sun goes down," gives him a wooden cup full of living water that is the sky—the power "to make live the greening day." He also gives him a bow that is the power to destroy.[39]

The Grandfather of the wintry North, where the "white giant" lives, gives Black Elk an herb of power that fattens a sick and starving horse. This grandfather says, "Take courage, younger brother. On earth a nation you shall make live, for yours shall be the power of the white giant's wing, the cleansing wing," that the people may have "endurance and face all winds with courage."[40]

The Grandfather of the East, where the daybreak star rises and the sun shines continually, gives Black Elk the sacred pipe, "the power that is peace and the good red day," saying, "with this pipe you shall walk upon the earth, and whatever sickens there you shall make well."[41]

The Grandfather of the South, "whence comes the power to grow," gives Black Elk a red stick that sprouts and becomes a great tree shading the happy "circled villages of people and every living thing with roots or legs or wings." This is the "sacred stick and the nation's hoop and the yellow day." "Younger brother," he says, "with the powers of the four quarters you shall walk, a relative. Behold, the living center of a nation I shall give you, and with it many you shall save. . . . It shall stand in the center of the nation's circle, a cane to walk with and a people's heart."[42]

The oldest of them all, the Grandfather of the Sky, becomes a spotted eagle and says, "Behold! all the wings of the air shall come to you and they and the winds and the stars shall be like relatives. You shall go across the earth with my power." And then the sky fills with friendly wings coming toward him.[43]

The sixth grandfather, the spirit of the Earth, slowly becomes a boy with Black Elk's face. When the grandfather is old again, he says, "My boy, have courage, for my power shall be yours, and you shall need it, for your nation on earth will have great troubles." Then Black Elk is shown the troubled future of his people: the broken hoop, the dying holy tree. He understands that the bison upon which his people depend will be taken away, but "from the same good spirit [his people] must find another strength." It will be the herb of understanding that bears four blossoms on a single stem—blue, white, red, and yellow, the colors of the four directions.[44]

At the end of his vision, Black Elk sees the whole universe dancing to the beautiful song of the black stallion. He sees "the shapes of all things in the spirit, and the shape of all shapes as they must live together like one being."[45] Thus Black Elk received the ancient vision of the universe as one vast interrelated organism, a vision Western science is only beginning to comprehend.

In his vision, Black Elk is given power over life and death, healing and purification, peace and nourishment. He is told that he is a relative to all things, even the winds and the stars, and that the power of the sky will aid him in his work. He sees that the spirit of the earth has a human face. This may be interpreted to mean that not only Black Elk, but all human beings, must, in their daily dealings with each other and the earth itself, strive to bring harmony to the natural and human world. The vision of Black Elk is, in this view, a vision in which humankind is reminded of its great potential for good and its responsibility as steward of the earth. Within its symbolism, the good red road crosses the black path of adversity at each point in space and time. By our every choice, we affirm or deny the life of the world, taking one path or the other. The voice that commanded Black Elk commands all people: "Behold this day, for it is yours to make."[46]

INVOKING THE POWERS

Remember, remember the circle of the sky
the stars and the brown eagle
the supernatural winds
breathing night and day
from the four directions

Remember, remember the great life of the sun
breathing on the earth
it lies upon the earth
to bring out life upon the earth
life covering the earth

Remember, remember the sacredness of things
running streams and dwellings
the young within the nest
a hearth for sacred fire
the holy flame of fire[47]

NOTES

1. Grandfather David Monongyne, letter to the United Nations General Assembly, in *New Age,* December 1982, p. 88.
2. T. C. McLuhan, ed., *Touch the Earth* (New York: Pocket Books, 1972), p. 2.
3. John G. Neihardt, *Black Elk Speaks* (New York: Pocket Books, 1972). Copyright © John G. Neihardt 1932, 1961, published by Simon & Schuster Pocket Books and the University of Nebraska Press, pp. 198–300.
4. Alice C. Fletcher, *The Hako: A Pawnee Ceremony.* Twenty-second annual report of the Bureau of American Ethnology to the Secretary of the Smithsonian Institution, 1900–1901, Part 2, J. W. Powell, Director. Smithsonian Institution, Washington, D.C. 1904. Reprinted by permission of Smithsonian Institution Press.
5. Nancy Wood, ed., *Hollering Sun* (New York: Simon & Schuster, 1972).

6. Chief Luther Standing Bear, *Land of the Spotted Eagles* (Boston: Houghton Mifflin, 1900), pp. 192–97.
7. McLuhan, p. 9.
8. Wood.
9. Dorothy Lee, *Freedom and Culture* (Englewood Cliffs, NJ: Prentice-Hall, 1959), p. 118.
10. Norman Russell, interview by Harris J. Elder, in Patrick D. Hundley, *The Magic of Names: Three Native American Poets* (Marvin, SD: Blue Cloud Quarterly Press, 1978).
11. John Bierhorst, ed., *In the Trail of the Wind: American Indian Poems and Ritual Orations* (New York: Farrar, Straus & Giroux, 1971), p. 124. Reprinted by permission of Farrar, Straus & Giroux, Inc.
12. Ibid., p. 19.
13. A Grove Day, *The Sky Clears: Poetry of the American Indians* (Lincoln: University of Nebraska Press, 1951), pp. 104–5. Reprinted by permission of the University of Nebraska Press. Copyright © 1951 by A. Grove Day.
14. Wood.
15. Ibid.
16. Brandon, ed., p. 43.
17. Day, pp. 109–10.
18. Wood.
19. Hyemeyohst Storm, *Seven Arrows* (New York: Ballantine, 1972), p. 6.
20. Frank Waters, *Book of the Hopi* (New York: Ballantine, 1963), p. xviii.
21. Ibid., p. 138.
22. Ibid., pp. 21–22, 27.
23. Ibid., p. 183.
24. Ibid., p. 33.
25. Ibid., p. 287.
26. Ibid., p. 10.
27. Ibid., pp. 165–66.
28. Ibid., p. 235.
29. Ibid., p. 33.
30. Ibid., p. 149.
31. Ibid., pp. 194–95.
32. Ibid., p. 198.
33. Ibid., p. 11.
34. Ibid., p. 211.
35. Neihardt, p. 2.
36. Ibid., p. 36.
37. Ibid., p. 232.
38. Storm, p. 221.
39. Neihardt, p. 26.
40. Ibid., pp. 23, 29.
41. Ibid., pp. 23, 26.
42. Ibid., pp. 24, 26.
43. Ibid., p. 25.
44. Ibid.
45. Ibid., pp. 35, 36.
46. Ibid., p. 35.
47. Brandon, p. 69.

· 10 ·

Buddhism:

A RELIGION OF STEWARDSHIP

IN recent years, the insights of Buddhism have begun to seep into the Western world. Since they are highly compatible with the ideas of stewardship, it will be useful to explore them here. Buddhism is not a revealed religion; those human beings who were there at its "root moments" did not see themselves as receiving a revelation from God. Instead, the truth of Buddhism is received through an experience of enlightenment within the individual which, according to adherents, liberates that individual from false assumptions about who and what we are. Our true self, it is argued, becomes buried under years of societal conditioning, but, with proper life-style and practice, we can regain the great freshness and clarity of our original nature.

Buddhism is not strongly dogmatic and does not claim exclusive truth. Because it is, in a sense, on a different plane from the revealed religions, many have found it compatible with them. Marian Mountain, in her book *The Zen Environment*, writes that a Buddhist teacher once told her that it was "easy for a Buddhist to be a Christian." At the same time, he cautioned that it is harder for a Christian to become a Buddhist.[1] But the life of the Catholic monk Thomas Merton shows that it is possible to strengthen one's Christian life through the study and practice of Buddhism.

Buddhism began in India in the sixth century B.C. and has since spread over much of Asia. Possibly one-quarter of the earth's population now follows some form of the Buddhist religion, and its intellectual influence is even more far-flung. The historic Buddha, Siddhartha Gautama, was the son of a rajah. As a young man, he became deeply aware of suffering in the world, left his privileged life behind, and became a seeker of the truth. After many years of self-denial and spiritual discipline, he received supreme enlightenment while sitting in meditation under a fig tree now known as the Bodhi Tree, or tree of wisdom.

Over and over it has been pointed out that to attempt to describe the content of mystical experience can be nothing more than a shadow game. Still, over and over, the attempt is made. Traditional Buddhist wisdom tells us that enlightenment releases us from the clutch of our personal ego. The supposedly enduring "self' is an illusion, actually coming together only during moments of personal awareness. We are, in fact—according to this thinking—nothing more than a bundle of thoughts and actions, becomings and extinctions, aggregates of memory. At the same time, we are one with everything else in the entire universe. Freed from attachment to an individual ego, Guatama Buddha and all future Buddhas—all human beings are considered to be latent Buddhas—became at that moment free from personal fear and desire. In this world of just-being, a great sense of liberation arises, as described in the following song from the *Dhammapada*:

> Vainly I sought the builder of my house
> Through countless lives.
> I could not find him. . . .
> How hard it is to tread life after life!
> But now I see you, O builder!
> And never again shall I build my house.
> I have snapped the rafters,
> Split the ridgepole
> And beaten out desire.
> Now my mind is free.[2]

At this moment the individual who has achieved enlightenment is immensely magnified. Nancy Wilson Ross, in *Buddhism, A Way of Life and Thought,* writes that "the horizon of the individual is extended to the very limits of reality, to a completely realized oneness. Nirvana is not to be equated with existentialism's abyss of annihilation, but instead to a boundless expansion. The image should not be the drop of water which merges into the ocean and is lost but rather the ocean which enters into the drop."[3]

This experience of oneness with a completely interconnected universe is, of course, fundamental also to our expanding ecological awareness. Modern physics, too, as its reality shifts from matter to energy, suggests such a picture of the universe. Couple this vision of oneness with the waning of greed that follows loss of the ego self—these are not just ideas, but deep changes within the individual being—and it becomes clear that Buddhism has great potential as a motivating force for stewardship. In *The Discourse on Universal Love*, the Buddha says, "As a mother, even at the risk of her own life, protects and loves her child, her only child, so let a man cultivate love without measure toward the whole world, above, below, and around, unmixed with any feeling of differing or opposing interests. Let a man remain steadfast in this state of mind all the while he is awake, whether he be standing, walking, sitting or lying down. This state of mind is the best in the world."[4]

The Buddhist poet Gary Snyder, in his book of essays *Earth House Hold*, writes of a three-level approach to Buddhist practice: "Wisdom . . . , meditation . . . , and morality . . . Wisdom is intuitive knowledge of the mind of love and clarity that lies beneath one's ego-driven anxieties and aggressions. Meditation is going into the mind to see this for yourself—over and over again, until it becomes the mind you live in. Morality is bringing it back out in the way you live, through personal example and responsible action, ultimately toward the true community (*sangha*) of 'all beings.' "[5]

The historic Buddha, Gautama, made a choice not to give himself up to the bliss of nirvana that follows upon enlightenment. Instead, in his love and compassion for this suffering world, he chose to stay and teach. Being not a god, but a man, however, with a very strange and revolutionary message, he found that this was not an easy road to walk. As with Christ in his more human moments, Gautama had moments of doubt and even anguish. Nancy Wilson Ross comments on this phenomenon of the Buddha's life: "One of the most famous of the

Chinese paintings of this particular moment in the buddha saga shows a tired, thin, shabby, even sad and anxious man standing on a windy slope, gazing down—with the all-too-human appearance of a person who has had his struggles and must now expect more—into the valley toward which he must travel to begin his mission."[6]

Gautama Buddha began his teaching with these four precepts: (1) Suffering is a condition of all existence; (2) suffering and general dissatisfaction come to human beings because they are possessive, greedy and, above all, self-centered; (3) egocentrism, possessiveness and greed can, however, be understood, overcome, rooted out; and (4) this rooting out can be brought about by following a simple, reasonable Eight-fold Path of behavior in thought, word and deed. Change of viewpoint will manifest itself in a new outlook and new patterns of behavior.[7]

The Eight-fold Path to solving "the human problem" entails right understanding, right purpose, right speech, right conduct, right livelihood, right effort, right awareness or mindfulness, and right concentration or meditation.[8]

Obviously the Eight-fold Path, too, when chosen by the individual who has been or is working to transcend his or her egotistical greed, is in the spirit of the highest standards of stewardship for our planet. In fact, among the followers of Buddhism, whose goal it is not to worship the Buddha, but to *become* a Buddha, many have made the same choice as did Gautama, to stay and serve. Such are known as Bodhisattvas.

The life of a Bodhisattva is not solely for followers of Buddhism. Such dedicated human beings as Mother Teresa, Mahatma Gandhi, Martin Luther King, Albert Schweitzer, and Hugh Bennett (an early "saint' of soil conservation in the United States) must surely be seen as having achieved this status. All of these great individuals have recognized their oneness with the greater whole and devoted their lives to its well-being.

Robert Aitken, in his book *Taking the Zen Path,* expanded on the Bodhisattva phenomenon: "The universe is one. How can you be enlightened unless all others are enlightened too? St. Paul said, 'The whole creation groaneth and travaileth in pain together until now.' The word 'travail' means the labor of childbirth. We are all of us involved in the great labor of the universe."[9]

The following vow—hopelessly beyond the reach of any mortal—is perhaps the most frequently chanted in the world of Buddhism:

> Though sentient beings are numberless,
> I vow to save them all;
> though the delusions of greed and hatred rise
> endlessly before us,
> I vow to end them all;
> though the gates of the Dharma are manifold,
> I vow to enter them all;
> though the Buddha's way is beyond attainment,
> I vow to attain it fully.[10]

The ideal of the individual's giving up himself or herself for the well-being of the larger whole is becoming more widely accepted in our contemporary world. Devoted cultural and environmental workers in the arts, sciences, and humanities are no longer uncommon, nor are socially conscious workers within the Christian tradition. Robert Aitken sees the Bodhisattva ideal—rather than a balanced budget or a technological breakthrough—as "our only hope for survival or indeed for the survival of any species. The three poisons of greed, hatred and ignorance are destroying our natural and cultural heritage. I believe that unless we as citizens of the world can take the radical Bodhisattva position, we will not even die with integrity."[11]

It may be that Buddhism has tended, more than most religions, to hold to the joy inherent in simplicity and hard work. Physical labor is honored in the Buddhist tradition. So, not surprisingly, is poverty. Marian Mountain writes that, "Poverty is the fundamental aspect of almost every religious teaching."[12] Mountain believes:

> The reason ordinary people can't find happiness in poverty is that they have been taught to fight poverty. But if we don't fight poverty, or ignore it, or run away from it—if we observe poverty with a mind free of preconceived ideas and false conditioning, poverty will reveal its true nature. The American writer-naturalist Thoreau extolled the value of a life of simplicity in his book

> *Walden Pond.* St. Francis of Assisi found a friend in poverty. He called his friend My Lady Poverty and wooed his Lady with courtly manners and troubadour songs. This kind of attitude is one in which we are able to appreciate fully the blessings of poverty.[13]

Mountain also quotes the Chinese Buddhist P'ang Chushi, in his enthusiasm for a simple life so characteristic of the Buddhist spirit: "Drawing water; carrying firewood; how wonderful, how mysterious!"[14] The citizens of a country such as the United States, who use so much more of the world's resources than their per capita share, might do well to consider this spirit.

Finally, in terms of land use, the Buddhist tradition has tended toward agrarianism. Its vision of the interconnected unity of all creation has been highly compatible with—if not in part responsible for—the highly productive, labor-intensive polyculture farms of eastern and southeastern Asia. Producing rice, vegetables, fish, and livestock in mutual interdependence, these farms reflect the ecological model for production that many of our more radical agricultural thinkers expect to be the approach Western agriculture, with modifications, will take in the future. The Oriental polycultural approach to farming has, when properly applied, proven its capacity to sustain high quality soils over many centuries. But more important than Buddhism's affinity for any given style of agriculture, is the awareness that lives increasingly in the minds of practicing Buddhists: that all human action in this fully interconnected world will, for good or evil, one day return to us. The Buddhist knows in his or her bones that in time we shall reap exactly as we sow.

NOTES

1. Marian Mountain, *The Zen Environment* (New York: Bantam Books, 1983), p. 77.
2. Thomas Byron, *The Dhammapada, the Sayings of the Buddha* (New York: Knopf, 1976), p. 56. Reprinted by permission of Alfred A. Knopf, Inc. Copyright © 1976 by Thomas Byron.

3. Nancy Wilson Ross, *Buddhism, A Way of Life and Thought* (New York: Vintage Books, 1981), p. 30. Reprinted by permission of Alfred A. Knopf, Inc. Copyright © 1980 by Nancy Wilson Ross.
4. Ibid., p. 32.
5. Gary Snyder, *Earth House Hold* (New York: New Directions, 1969), p. 92. Reprinted by permission of New Directions Publishing Company, © 1969 by Gary Snyder.
6. Ross, p. 18.
7. Ibid., p. 23.
8. Ibid., p. 24.
9. Robert Aitken, *Taking the Path of Zen* (Berkeley, CA: North Point Press, 1982), p. 62. Excerpted from *Taking the Path of Zen,* published by North Point Press and reprinted by permission. All rights reserved. Copyright © 1982 by Diamond Sangha.
10. Ibid.
11. Ibid.
12. Mountain, p. 102–3.
13. Ibid., p. 162.
14. Ibid., p. 163.

· 11 ·

Grounding:

A FEMINIST VIEW OF LAND STEWARDSHIP

WE in the West have never stopped trying to rise above the earth. Towers, skyscrapers, rockets, mountain climbs, moon walks, voyages to probe the mysteries of deep space. The Western mind, likewise, soars from concrete reality into the abstractions of language, science, philosophy, the nation-state, the multinational corporation, the hierarchies of institutional religion. Spiritually, too, we try to escape the earth. Transcendent gods, the soul split from the body, ascensions into heaven. The earth is the given, the ground against which marches the multifaceted figure of our quest for more. What *is* is never enough. What is *not* calls us to conquest and dominion, regardless or perhaps because of danger.

The attempt to rise above what is, to transcend and dominate reality—a predominantly male preoccupation—has been criticized by feminists. They point out that except for the goddess-worshipping, earth-centered, and perhaps mythological matriarchies of prehistory, the cultures of the earth have been male-dominated. In countless myths, worldwide, males have seen earth as the mother from—and against which—the son, as hero, must rise.[1] The history of the West chronicles that attempt to rise. We do not know what forms of culture a matriarchy might have created, but we do know that the abstract, linear, control-oriented approach of our dominant culture keeps us out of balance. Its excesses threaten to topple the very structures it builds. The earth groans under the weight of greed and waste and sickens with poisons. We cannot rise in linear "progress" fast enough to escape the consequences of our actions.[2]

Perhaps no aspect of our dominant culture is more exaggeratedly "masculine," more out of balance, than technological agriculture. Even in this most earthy of enterprises, we struggle to rise above the earth. We need look no farther than the four-wheel-drive tractors, with their air conditioned cabs and stereo music that separate many of today's farmers from the dust and heat of field work, to see how the industrial model permeates the modern farm. It extends to the treatment of animals as well. Caged chickens, tranquilized against savaging one another, are stacked in "skyscrapers." The feet of confined hogs never touch the ground. A chemical or mechanical solution, applied on schedule, is sought for every problem. Airplanes buzz the land, spraying pesticides. Fields are plowed according to the abstractions of property lines, geometry, and the dimensions of machines. The force of gravity on water and soil, the action of wind across plowed ground, are seldom considered. Indeed, many scientists dream of a hydroponic agriculture that will, like a space station, finally dispense with earth altogether. Here all processes will be monitored and controlled in a triumph of scientific method, all mystery laid open and dissected in the bright light of reason.

But animals and growing plants and soil are natural systems that do not necessarily fit our rational constructs of the way things *should* work. Every action creates a reaction. We never know enough to control every variable. The source of life remains a mystery. In order to be truly healthy and sustainable, truly practical, systems must work in harmony with nature. Our survival depends upon a change of heart. We must bring our technology, our institutions, our ideas, our spirituality, and certainly our agriculture back to earth. We must again become *grounded.*

Feminism, in its radical critique of male-dominated culture, provides a vision that seeks to balance our relationship to the earth, to let us rise in flights of art and science but remain, at the same time, grounded in acceptance of the way of things. It asserts that our problems lie not only in the fact that women have not shared power equally with men, but in our overly masculine orientation. Elizabeth Dodson Gray writes that humankind was born a twin and the male approach is only half of the picture.[3] Our "truth" has been in fact a "masculinist" interpretation of reality. Many feminists believe that we must see the other half too if we are to approach truth. We must reach out for what we can learn from post-patriarchal women if we are ever to reach our full human potential. Indeed, some believe we may not survive unless we make the life-supporting values traditionally held by women our first priority.

In splitting matter from spirit, body from mind, earth from heaven, the Judeo-Christian tradition that permeates Western culture has given priority to spirit, mind, and heaven. Consciously or unconsciously, women have been identified with the rejected portion. The earth has been mythologized as female and, like women, has been a prime target for domination.[4] The body, partaking as it does of earth, has all too often been viewed as something to be transcended rather than nurtured. And the everyday realities of life-maintenance have been almost universally assigned a low status and left to women.[5] In the hierarchy that we impose on the world, God rules men, who in turn rule women, children, animals, and plants. At the very bottom lies the silent earth,[6] the mother, source of passive receptiveness and endless bounty.

As we have made clear elsewhere in this book, feminism is not alone in its condemnation of the aggressive values of the dominant culture. A worldwide undercurrent of dissent whispers of the emptiness of exploitation, the poverty of the pursuit of worldly goods, the impotence of power. Tribal peoples, mystics, environmentalists, poets, and artists proclaim our need for a harmonious relationship with nature. But the most dominating and exploitative elements have nearly always held sway, seeking to destroy, or at least discredit, all those—women and men—who would speak for the earth.

Among others, Anne Wilson Schaef has posited a "women's reality," both opposing and complementary to the dominant masculine. Largely ignored by men and confined historically to the women's sphere, this approach is characterized by relationship rather than estrangement, cooperation instead of competition, nurture and service in place of domination. It seeks to understand the world through empathetic observation rather than by dissection and experimentation. It trusts and works in harmony with natural processes, rather than imposing upon them an abstract, rational, human-centered control.

"Feminine" thought processes are, in this view, intuitive—comfortable with ambiguity and paradox—not bound by the constraints of either/or rationality. They are process- rather than product-oriented.[7] Whether or not these qualities are always attributable to women, they have been largely absent, at least until recently, from science, philosophy, theology, and business. Only rarely have they been applied to agriculture.

The terms *masculine* and *feminine* in this context do not refer to men and women as such. They are abstractions, cultural paradigms. By their very nature they are exaggerations. They are useful here because our dominant culture has made a deep rift between them, as exemplified in our sex-role stereotypes and in our basic approaches to the world. We see *masculine* as active and dominant and *feminine* as receptive and submissive. These generalizations have led many men—and women—to attenuate aspects of themselves accordingly. But just as our society is made up of a vast array of racial, ethnic, and ideational groups, so too are men and women made up of clusters of traits and qualities that cannot be neatly classified as masculine or feminine. It is perhaps dangerous to even speak in such terms. But if our dominant culture were to incorporate culturally feminine qualities, not only would the rift between the sexes be lessened, but it is likely our approach to the earth would also become more balanced.

In examining the masculine orientation of modern agriculture, it may be useful to look at how women have related to it. Anthropologists suggest that the women of ancient times, in order to assure a more dependable food supply, invented agriculture. Historically, women have everywhere done a large share of farm work. In the United States, however, agriculture is one of the most male-dominated professions, with women making up only 5 percent of the sole proprietors of farms.[8] Studies suggest that in a husband-wife partnership, the wife's role in decision-making is unclear,[9] but it is likely that the man makes most major decisions, including those relating to the care of land. A woman may perform any and all farm tasks, may keep the books or take charge of certain operations, but in popular parlance her husband is the "farmer." She is the "farmer's wife." He is "working"; she is "helping." In the soil conservation district, too, he volunteers as a soil supervisor and she becomes a member of the ladies auxilliary. Involved in their work and frequently isolated, farm women have tended to defer their individual goals in favor of the well-being of the family farm.[10]

For all their strength and resiliency, farm women have usually identified with their husbands' points of view. At times, in fact, it seems as if many have abdicated their responsibility to take a stand on large issues whether it be arms control or the use of pesticides. Although their views are often not taken seriously, women should not be absolved for confining themselves to the narrow world of the household. Part of nurturing children is making sure they have a safe world in which to live. Part of feeding them is protecting the source of that food, the land. Ideally there is no separation between the personal and public sphere. As poet Gary Snyder points out, the Greek root for both ecology and economics means "household."[11]

It is not that farm women have ignored values. Quite the contrary. Christina Gladwin of the University of Florida writes that farm women have always directed much of their energy toward transmitting to their children the values that help the family farm survive.[12] And historian Joan M. Jensen makes clear that rural women have created a culture of support for one another and their communities that has allowed them to handle welfare activities, create schools and cultural organizations, and organize political and community action.[13]

In the farm crisis of this decade, farm women have overcome their rural isolation to organize, demonstrate, and run for office—in the main to save the family farm. Films such as *Country* have even shown farm women fighting alone, unsupported by men. A leading spokesperson of "Groundswell," a farm resistance group in Minnesota, is a farm woman, as were several leaders of an extended protest against a rural power line. These women may well gain strength from the idea that women need not bury their pain and anger beneath a facade of stoicism. Feeling, which we tend to identify as feminine, must in such times be expressed. Certainly the episodes of farmers killing bankers and themselves show the explosiveness of rage and fear that are unexpressed.

In its extremity, the farm crisis can no longer be dealt with from the traditionally masculine perspectives of economics and competition. Poet Meridel LeSueur whose eighty-some years have been spent battling for the earth and all oppressed beings, says the patriarchy, the rule of the fathers, is dying, destroying itself for lack of nourishment. But, she adds, a new birth is inevitable, and women are the seed of the transformation of the earth.[14]

Although activist farm women have certainly taken a stand, it is the family as a unit and the farm as an economic, not an ecological entity that they strive to save. This fierce protection of a way of life and livelihood has not usually been extended to the source of that life, the land. Not many have sought to save the farm by saving the soil.

Urban women are even farther removed from the everyday realities of farmland. In our predominantly urban society, acres of concrete and asphalt, manicured lawns, disposals, toilets, plastic bags, and prepackaged microwavable meals create an artificial reality. Rural concerns seem remote. There are, of course, some who seek a "natural" life-style within the city—who attempt to limit their consumption of material goods, recycle wastes, search out unprocessed and organic food. But even their contact with and understanding of farmland is at best limited. City dwellers depend on others to grow their food, others who may or may not protect the land in the process.[15]

Many urban women have taken on the major causes of our day. Those who are environmentalists often work to save endangered animals such as whales or harp seal pups, to protect virgin forests or marshes, or to stop pollution, waste, or nuclear energy. But not until recently has farmland, this most basic human habitat, surfaced in the consciousness of more than a few environmentalists. It is as though farmland were only what we drive through to get to the scenery.

If asked, of course, urban environmentalists would agree on the importance of soil conservation, but they do not often put it high on their list of issues. The rural/urban split in American culture runs almost as deep as the split between matter and spirit, indeed is part of that split. Our national agenda, as reflected in legislation, public policy discussions, and in the media, is urban.[16] The 97 percent of us who are not farmers have to work to discover our connection to the land. It is too easy for us to drift on in a technological bubble as though soil resources were infinite. The lack of a consensus for conservation allows farmers to ignore the erosion they see daily, and to continue their power struggle with the land.

The women's movement expresses concepts that could remedy our approach to farmland. One of its most compelling themes, political power as based in spirituality, has resulted in a new definition of power. Miriam Simos distinguishes between the *power-over*, identified as masculine, and the *power-from-within* she finds awakening in modern women. She believes our civilization has been built on a hierarchical power over others, a power that rests on alienation, the world separated into entities we dominate and manipulate. Such power can lead only to destruction.[17]

But Simos and others sense, deep within us and within all life, a different sort of power, one that unfolds in growth and ripening. This life force or spirit—what Charlene Spretnak calls "elemental power"[18]—creates, heals, sustains and connects all things.[19] All life-forms continually seek to become whole and fully realized. This is the meaning of life. When we ally with this power we commit ourselves to continual growth and change—of our selves and all things. Trusting this power that creates in its own time, women and men may not be tempted to violate natural development, to interrupt cycles so as to try to tear flower from bud or apple from blossom. We may feel our life to be an expression of all life.

In empowering themselves as individuals, feminists have explored new ways for groups, too, to deal with power. By making the group process conscious, they acknowledge the importance of process itself. In women's support groups, decisions are frequently made by consensus. The matrix is not power-over, not "winning through intimidation," but a true democracy that nurtures the intrinsic value of each member. In the process of cooperation necessary to reach consensus, a whole is expressed that is larger than the sum of its parts.

Farming, which has usually been a power-over enterprise, a long-standing competition with natural forces or with others in the marketplace, could benefit from the incorporation of a feminist approach to power. The farmer's goal has typically been to extract from land as much as possible despite the limitations imposed by climate, weather, soil type, and insect and weed populations. What if farmers attended to process as well as product? What if they adopted a cooperative approach and considered the well-being of the farm as a whole and of each of its aspects? What if farmers trusted the elemental power of nature within the soil? The goal of such farmers would be to help the land to reach its optimum health. Rather than imposing, by force of will, a preconceived plan, they would try to further what is already there.

A few such farmers exist. Like the husbandman of land described by Wendell Berry, they have developed their allegedly feminine qualities of nurturance and relationship.[20] Not only is this beneficial to land, it is also ultimately easier. So much of the toil of farming is unnecessary—what ridge-till advocate Ernest Behn calls "recreational farming."[21] Many farmers have found that their tillage work does little to increase yields and in fact serves to lay the land bare to wind and water. And erosion makes necessary further work. Slopes washed out by spring rains must be replanted, and gullies mended to prevent damage to machines. Fencelines drifted in with soil must be cleaned out. Farmers must also bear the enormous psychic burden of trying to still the voice deep within that whispers of something beyond economic "bottom line."

Relationship is another supposedly feminine quality, the ability to bond with places, animals, children, spouses, other family members, friends. This bonding helps hold civilization together and may help to control and temper aggressiveness. Although feminism seeks to reclaim for women some measure of aggressiveness, at its best, it does so within a context of relatedness. In recent years, in fact, many feminists have in ritual, poetry, and political action "aggressively" celebrated their relationship with the earth. They seem to feel in continuum with the earth's great body. In this view, our lives rise out of the earth and sink back in. We *are* the earth, in continual communion with it. In caring for the earth we care for our own flesh.

Such celebration may be feminine, but it is not exclusive to women. Neither is it a mere mental appreciation or ethical decision: it is a felt relationship, an unconditional acceptance of what is, after all, scientific fact. When we celebrate the basic conditions of life, we transform our experience. The world is valued for what it *is* rather than for what it could become or what could be extracted from it. When we abandon the expectations and projections that obscure the world, it becomes beautiful to us, its wonder revealed.[22] We develop an empathy that enables us, like the Wintu woman quoted by T. C. McLuhan, to feel the pain and pleasure of the ecosystem.

Several years ago a television documentary pictured Dian Fossey in the bush with a family of gorillas. Fossey, using the method Jane Goodall had pioneered with chimpanzees, mimicked the gorillas' behavior, breakng off stems and pretending to eat the leaves. The gorillas had apparently come to accept her as a harmless addition to the group. She was a *scientist,* but her method was noninvasive. It did not "murder to dissect"; the whole system of the life of this gorilla family remained intact. Thus the observer was able to truly know them in their natural state. And they were surprisingly gentle. One young male, after perhaps months of cautious approach, actually reached out his hairy but almost human hand to touch hers.

It is probably no coincidence that this scientist was a woman, or that her gentle approach made such contact possible. Study of a caged or dissected animal tells little about its life in the wild. A living being can be known only if left intact.

Similarly, the intrusive and reductive method of modern agricultural science cannot discover the true nature of living soil. Dissected and analyzed, soil seems a conglomeration of separate elements, all easily replaceable by scientific intervention. If soil erodes, the roots of plants can be bathed in chemical equivalents of soil nutrients and held by crushed rock. A feminine approach to agriculture, on the other hand, would intuit a greater complexity and wholeness in a natural system than even our most sophisticated techniques can ferret out. Patiently observing that system, such farmers would try to mimic and fit into it. They would also be willing to let it be. In empathy, not control, they would intervene only to guide or prevent harm.[23]

What if we actually viewed agricultural land with empathy? What if we extended to land the nurture we give children? Would we *feel* the damage visited upon that land? Would we discover, at last, the full meaning of the human role: to sense, comprehend, and reestablish harmony on earth?

To seek harmony is not to try to vanquish the pain and death that lie at the very heart of natural process. Like all natural processes, agriculture, too, depends on death. In most forms of farming, chosen plants are nurtured; the rest are cultivated out, turned under to replenish soil. Only what grows in the straight rows of our design may reach toward light. But modern agriculture inserts technology between the poles of life and death. Modern agriculture does not manage this cycle, but attempts to transcend it. What it kills all too often feeds nothing. Even its feeding kills. Its fertilizers burn the living soil to produce surplus. Washing from the fields, they stimulate the growth of algae, which choke lakes. Pesticides, which suggest our distrust of natural process, escape our control and return through streams and groundwater to sicken us. A feminine agriculture would intuitively recognize that the water cycle, the bloodstream of the planet, is not separate from our own. It would understand that if the foods that become our bodies are the products of diminished soil, our lives will be likewise diminished.

If agriculture needs a feminine approach, what then should be the role of women in bringing that about? Historically, women have been the feeders, the nurturers.[24] In the tradition-based past of agricultural societies, women grew and gathered most of the food supply. In many parts of the Third World, women today still do.[25] And in the United States, despite efforts to escape sex-role stereotypes, women are likely to purchase and cook, if not produce, the food that feeds their families. Within marriages or as heads of single-parent households, women seem to be inexplicably tied to nurture.

Whether this is due to the expectations of men, the needs of children, or some inherent quality of women remains to be seen. Some women embrace the role; others reject it as limiting, perhaps themselves wishing to rise above the earth and its complex cycle from soil to dinner table and back again. These women might also see the idea that they extend their nurturing to land as just one more request for women to clean up after men.[26] In any event, even with the conservation efforts of a few women and men, male-dominated agriculture is not adequately caring for land. Women have been in the forefront of other survival issues, and farmland preservation is most assuredly a survival issue. Women must insist that all of us—men as well as women—become nurturers of the land.

This will not be an easy task. Soil does not *easily* excite the modern mind. To most it seems silent and motionless, dead, boring. Our bond with soil goes as deep as life and death, but often fails to surface in our awareness. The peasant women of India place their newborns on the ground and banish evil by pressing a thumbprint of dirt to the baby's forehead,[27] but we keep our babies clean, free of dirt. Though some love the feel of soil between their fingers, many shrink from it as if to avoid the death it carries. Detergent ads promise protection from "soiled" clothing. To "soil one's hands" means to damage one's character. In a balanced culture "soiling one's hands" would perhaps mean having a close connection with the earth, and it would be a good thing, not a liability.

In a nurturing agriculture, feminine qualities would further the wholeness of the land. Farmers would, like ideal mothers, understand their welfare to be identical with that of the land. As far as possible they would cultivate natural processes: diversity rather than monoculture; integrated pest management instead of scheduled spraying; rotation, cover crops, and green manure instead of chemicals; shelterbelts, terraces, and conservation tillage done on the contour would be sharp contrast to the bare, eroding fields of our agricultural desert. These techniques are known, and they work. We only have to change our minds and hearts.

At the darkest moment of the winter, the longest night, the light begins its return. That is the way of all nature: renewal follows decay. Out of poisoned ground eventually sprouts the new green plants whose life will heal that ground. Out of our despair at the imbalances in modern agriculture must come also hope for change. And it is out of the barrenness created by competitive domination that a feminine approach to agriculture will be born. Change will come not from those who have adopted the dominant paradigm but from those who have created a new definition of strength that is grounded in the life-energy of the earth.[28]

The low status we give to the tasks of life maintenance is the exact index of our alienation from the earth. Many women have understandably desired liberation from these tasks. For most farmers, too, soil conservation, the life maintenance of the very ground of agriculture, is its least considered element. But it is a poor liberation that leaves life support in neglectful hands. By expanding to the land the nurture we give within our families, women and men, urban and rural, could help to correct these priorities. This means insisting, by whatever means, that farmers, legislators, agriculture professionals, corporate landholders, bankers, even consumers, make care of land an integral part of all dealings with it.

In this context, the feminist axiom that "the personal is political" reveals another aspect of its meaning: the nurturing that has always been denigrated as impractical, uneconomic, or unscientific must become public policy. Men must abandon their urge to dominate and compete with land. And women must abolish the "ladies' auxiliary" syndrome and see themselves as central, no longer confined by patriarchal definitions. Just as many women have taken responsibility for their own lives and bodies, they must take their share of responsibility for their extended body, the land.

But what does this mean in a time when corporations increasingly control land; when we are divided, urban from rural, environmentalist from consumer? These times require a transformation whose form and development remain to be seen. The peace quilts and marches, the leaflets, protests, and sit-ins, the peace encampments, the webs strung across the entrances to power, the chants and rituals with which we have made peace may point the way. Perhaps the feminist vision will truly help us to make peace with the land, to "reweave the web of life."[29] Perhaps women and men will stop trying to transcend the earth and find a transcendant meaning immanent within our lives on this planet. Humankind's greatest "conquest" may well be the establishment of harmony on earth. What better way to use the life-energy that flows freely into us out of the ground than to heal that ground?

NOTES

1. Elizabeth Dodson Gray, *Green Paradise Lost* (Wellesley, MA: Roundtable Press, 1979), p. 42.
2. Sonjie Johnson, "A Conversation with Meridel LeSueur," *Plainswomen* November/December 1979, p. 7.
3. Gray, p. 150.
4. Ibid., pp. 30–42.
5. Joan Dye Gussow, "Women and Food," *Country Journal*, February 1985.
6. Gray, p. 4.
7. Anne Wilson Schaef, *Women's Reality: An Emerging Female System in the White Male Society* (Minneapolis: Winston, 1981), p. 138.
8. Joan M. Jensen, ed., *With These Hands* (New York: Feminist Press, 1981).
9. Peggy J. Ross, "A Commentary on Research on American Farm Women," *Agriculture and Human Values*, Winter 1985, p. 27.
10. Joan M. Jensen, "The Role of Farm Women in American History: Areas for Additional Research," *Agriculture and Human Values*, Winter 1985, p. 13.
11. Gary Synder, *Earth House Hold* (New York: New Directions, 1969).

12. Christina Gladwin, "Values and Goals of Florida Farm Women: Do They Help the Family Farm Survive?" *Agriculture and Human Values*, Winter 1985, p. 45.
13. Jensen, pp. 13–17.
14. Johnson, p. 7.
15. Gussow.
16. Victor Ray, "Survival and the Urban Ethic," *Catholic Rural Life*, July 1985, pp. 17–18.
17. Miriam Simos (Starhawk), *Dreaming the Dark: Magic, Sex and Politics* (Boston: Beacon Press, 1982), pp. 3, 5.
18. Charlene Spretnak, ed., *The Politics of Women's Spirituality* (Garden City, NY: Anchor Press/Doubleday, 1982), p. xiii.
19. Simos, p. 4.
20. Wendell Berry, *The Unsettling of America* (San Francisco: Sierra Club Books, 1978), p. 8.
21. Ernest E. Behn, *More Profit with Less Tillage* (Des Moines, IA: Wallace-Homestead, 1982), p. 16.
22. Miriam and Jose Arguelles, *The Feminine: Spacious As the Sky* (Boulder, CO: Shambhala Publications, 1977), p. 24.
23. Jeremy Rifkin, in Philip Zaleski and Peggy Taylor, "Conversations with a Heretic," *New Age Journal*, November 1985, p. 83.
24. Gussow.
25. Anita Spring and Art Hanson, "The Underside of Development," *Agriculture and Human Values*, Winter 1985, p. 61.
26. Susan Griffin, *Women and Nature* (New York: Harper Colophon Books, 1978), p. xv.
27. David Suzuki, "A Planet for the Taking," television documentary, Public Broadcasting System, December 19, 1985.
28. Hallie Iglehart, *Womanspirit, A Guide to Women's Wisdom* (San Francisco: Harper & Row, 1983), pp. xii, 1.
29. Pam McAlister, ed., *Reweaving the Web of Life: Feminism and Nonviolence* (Philadelphia: New Society, 1982).

· 12 ·

Perspectives on Land Stewardship

THIS chapter gathers excerpts from the work of writers concerned with the environment. These selections have been arranged to flow one piece to the next within five sections: The Soil, Soil Erosion, Land Appropriated for Development, Relationship to Nature, and Stewardship. To us this seems a helpful way to present a concentration of high-quality thinking on our subject.

The Soil

CAREY McWILLIAMS
As the soil blows away or is washed away, the relation of the people to the land becomes increasingly tenuous. The people, in time, become badly "eroded" themselves. They lack capital; they lack education and training; they lack medical care and attention. (From *Ill Fares the Land,* New York: Barnes and Noble, 1942.)

WES JACKSON
[During the long history of life on earth] an important system was developing literally under the feet of diverse life forms. The early dust of the earth was mostly cemented together. It gradually became pulverized by the action of wind and water, plant roots and gravity. The bodies of dead plants and animals were added to this powder. A peculiar type of evolution was under way. This entity teemed with small organisms which

secreted chemicals into the powder. Small life forms ingested and egested it, buffered it and burrowed in it. It grew in thickness and began to cover a large area with what we might call "ecological capital." The capital of soil creates "interest" in the form of more soil. This interest then becomes reinvested. Water and wind still carried tons of this capital to the sea to become sedimentary layers, as it always had, but the life forms seemed almost purposefully devoted to retarding this work of gravity. From one point of view, David Brower has humorously suggested, plants and animals were evolved by this soil system to save itself and further its own spread.

A book written in 1905 by Harvard professor Nathaniel Southgate Sahler entitled *Man and Earth* described the soil and water system as an enveloping membrane or film, a placenta, through which the Earth mother sustains life. All life, including humans, Sahler suggested, draws life from the sun, clouds, air and earth through this living film. If the placenta is not kept healthy or intact, life above suffers. If healthy, it is a rich, throbbing support system. His message was clear enough: protect the placenta and you protect all Nature's children.

Placenta may not be the best word, for once a birth is complete the placenta is disposed of. And yet Mother Earth is always pregnant with new life and therefore an intact placenta is necessary. Perhaps a better word is matrix. To the biologist a matrix is something within which something else originates or develops. In archaic Latin, matrix means uterus or womb; the word is derived from mater or mother. But this is the age of the computer and now the word is associated with the computer. Call it what you will, soil is important not just for land life but for life in the ocean around the continental shelves. In fact, the open ocean is a desert. It would seem as if all life forms—except plants—take this system for granted, regarding it much as they would regard gravity. When humans arrived, they, like the other animals, paid it no special respect. (From *New Roots for Agriculture,* San Francisco: Friends of the Earth/Land Institute, 1980.)

ALDO LEOPOLD

That man is, in fact, only a member of a biotic team is shown by an ecological interpretation of history. Many historical events, hitherto explained solely in terms of human enterprise, were actually biotic interactions between people and land. The characteristics of the land determined the facts quite as potently as the characteristics of the men who lived on it.

Consider, for example, the settlement of the Mississippi valley. In the years following the Revolution, three groups were contending for its control: the native Indian, the French and English traders, and the American settlers. Historians wonder what would have happened if the English at Detroit had thrown a little more weight into the Indian side of those tipsy scales which decided the outcome of the colonial migration into the cane-lands of Kentucky. It is time now to ponder the fact that the cane-lands, when subjected to the particular mixture of forces represented by the cow, plow, fire, and axe of the pioneer, became bluegrass. What if the plant succession inherent in this dark and bloody ground had, under the impact of these forces, given us some worthless sedge, shrub, or weed? Would Boone and Kenton have held out? Would there have been any overflow into Ohio, Indiana, Illinois, and Missouri? Any Louisiana Purchase? Any transcontinental union of new states? Any Civil War? (From *A Sand County Almanac with Essays from Round River*, New York: Ballantine, 1970.)

VILHELM MOBERG

Karl Oskar mused to himself that probably he was the first white man ever to go through the forest at this place. . . . He felt as though this soil had been lying here waiting just for him. It had been waiting for him while he, in another land, had broken stone and more stone, laid it in piles and built fences with it, broken his equipment on it; all the while this earth had waited for him, while he had wasted his strength on roots and stones; his father had labored to pile the stone heaps higher and higher, to build the fences longer and broader, had broken himself on the stones so that now he must hobble along crippled, on a pair of crutches for the rest of his life—while all this earth had been lying here waiting. While his father sacrificed his good healthy legs for the spindly blades that grew among the stones at home, this deep, fertile soil had nurtured wild grass, harvested by no one. It had been lying here useless, sustaining not a soul. This rich soil without a stone in it had lain here since the day it was created, waiting for its tiller.

Now he had arrived. . . . (From *Unto a Good Land*, New York: Simon & Schuster, 1954.)

ALDO LEOPOLD

In Germany there is a mountain called the Spessart. Its south slope bears the most magnificent oaks in the world. American cabinetmakers, when they want the last word in quality, use Spessart oak. The north slope, which should be the better, bears an indifferent stand of Scotch pine. Why? Both slopes are part of the same state forest; both have been managed with equally scrupulous care for two centuries. Why the difference?

Kick up the litter under the oak and you will see that the leaves rot almost as fast as they fall. Under the pines, though, the needles pile up as a thick duff; decay is much slower. Why? Because in the Middle Ages the south slope was preserved as a deer forest by a hunting bishop; the north slope was pastured, plowed, and cut by settlers, just as we do with our woodlots in Wisconsin and Iowa today. Only after this period of abuse was the north slope replanted to pines. During this period of abuse something happened to the microscopic flora and fauna of the soil. The number of species was greatly reduced, i.e., the digestive apparatus of the soil lost some of its parts. Two centuries of conservation have not sufficed to restore these losses. It required the modern microscope, and a century of research in soil science, to discover the existence of these "small cogs and wheels" which determine harmony or disharmony between men and land in the Spessart. (From *A Sand County Almanac.*)

WENDELL BERRY

The soil is the great connector of lives, the source and destination of all. It is the healer and restorer and resurrector, by which disease passes into health, age into youth, death into life. Without proper care for it we can have no community, because without proper care for it we can have no life.

It is alive itself. It is a grave, too, of course. Or a healthy soil is. It is full of dead animals and plants, bodies that have passed through other bodies. For except for some humans—with their sealed coffins and vaults, their pathological fear of the earth—the only way into the soil is through other bodies. But no matter how finely the dead are broken down, or how many times they are eaten, they yet give into other life. If a healthy soil is full of death it is also full of life: worms, fungi, microorganisms of all kinds, for which, as for us humans, the dead bodies of the once living are a feast. Eventually this dead matter becomes soluble, available as food for plants, and life begins to rise up again out of the soil into the light. Given only the health of the soil, nothing that dies is dead for very long. Within this powerful economy, it seems that death occurs only for the good of life. (From *The Unsettling of America.* Copyright 1977 by Wendell Berry. Reprinted by permission of Sierra Club Books.)

Soil Erosion

EUGENE M. POIROT

A margin of life is developed by Nature for all living things—including man. All life forms obey Nature's demands—except man, who has found ways of ignoring them. For a brief historical time, this violation of Nature's laws has served to his advantage. In the long run it will destroy him. Starvation all over the world is evidence of the final result. In the United States, we are far from starvation, yet the symptoms of our violations are clearly evident: the loss of wildlife, muddy streams, bankrupt farmers leaving the land, consumers complaining about the high cost of food and steady environmental deteriorations. (From *Our Margin of Life,* Raytown, MO: Acres U.S.A., 1978.)

HAMLIN GARLAND

Again we went forth on the land, this time to wrestle with the tough, unrotted sod of the new breaking, while all around us the larks and plover called and the gray badgers stared with disapproving bitterness from their ravaged hills.

Maledictions on that tough northwest forty! How many times I harrowed and cross-harrowed it I cannot say, but I well remember the maddening persistency with which the masses of hazel roots clogged the teeth of the drag, making it necessary for me to raise the corner of it—a million times a day! This had to be done while the team was in motion, and you can see I did not lack for exercise. It was necessary also to "laphalf" and this requirement made careful driving needful for Father could not be fooled. He saw every "balk."

As the ground dried off the dust arose from under the teeth of the harrow and flew so thickly that my face was not only coated with it but tears of rebellious rage stained my cheeks with comic lines. At such times it seemed unprofitable to be the twelve-year-old son of a western farmer.

One day, just as the early sown wheat was beginning to throw a tinge of green over the brown earth, a tremendous wind arose from the southwest and blew with such devastating fury that the soil, caught up from the field, formed a cloud, hundreds of feet high—a cloud which darkened the sky, turning noon into dusk and sending us all to shelter. All the forenoon this blizzard of loam raged, filling the house with dust, almost smothering the cattle in the stable. Work was impossible, even for the men. The growing grain, its roots exposed to the air, withered and died. Many of the smaller plants were carried bodily away.

As the day wore on Father fell into dumb, despairing rage. His rigid face and smoldering eyes, his grim lips, terrified us all. It seemed to him (as to us), that the entire farm was about to take flight and the bitterest part of the tragic circumstance lay in the reflection that our loss (which was much greater than any of our neighbors) was due to the extra care with which we had pulverized the ground.

"If only I hadn't gone over it that last time," I heard him groan in reference to the "smooch" with which I had crushed all the lumps making every acre friable as a garden. "Look at Woodring's!" Sure enough. The cloud was thinner over on Woodring's side of the line fence. His rough clods were hardly touched. My father's bitter revolt, his impotent fury appalled me, for it seemed to me (as to him), that nature was, at the moment, an enemy. More than seventy acres of this land had to be resown. (From *Son of the Middle Border.* Copyright 1917 by Hamlin Garland. New York: Macmillan, 1924. Reprinted with permission of the publisher.)

JOHN STEINBECK

The dawn came, but no day. In the gray sky a red sun appeared, a dim circle that gave a little light, like dusk; and as that day advanced, the dusk slipped back toward darkness, and the wind cried and whimpered over the fallen corn.

Men and women huddled in their houses, and they tied handkerchiefs over their noses when they went out, and wore goggles to protect their eyes.

When the night came again it was black night, for the stars could not pierce the dust to get down, and the window lights could not even spread beyond their own yards. Now the dust was evenly mixed with the air, an emulsion of dust and air. Houses were shut tight, and cloth wedged around doors and windows, but the dust came in so thinly that it could not be seen in the air, and it settled like pollen on the chairs and tables, on the dishes. The people brushed it from their shoulders. Little lines of dust lay at the door sills. . . .

The people came out of their houses and smelled the hot stinging air and covered their noses from it. And the children came out of the houses, but they did not run or shout as they would have done after a rain. Men stood by their fences and looked at the ruined corn, drying fast now, only a little green showing through the film of dust. The men were silent and they did not move often. And the women came out of the houses to stand beside their men—to feel whether this time the men would break. The women studied the men's faces secretly, for the corn could go, as long as something else remained. The children stood near by, drawing figures in the dust with bare toes, and the children sent exploring senses out to see whether men and women would break. The children peeked at the faces of the men and women, and then drew careful lines in the dust with their toes. Horses came to the watering troughs and nuzzled the water to clear the surface dust. After a while the faces of the watching men lost their bemused perplexity and became hard and angry and resistant. (From *The Grapes of Wrath.* Copyright 1939, renewed © 1967 by John Steinbeck. Reprinted by permission of Viking Penguin, Inc.)

VICTOR K. RAY

From May 9 to 12, 1934, the most massive dust storm in history swept out of the drought-stricken breadbasket of the United States. Airplane flights out of Chicago had to be cancelled. Street lights were on at midday. The dust storm did not settle until it was far out in the Atlantic Ocean. The Associated Press estimated that 300 million tons of topsoil were removed from American farms.

As it happened, the Congress was at the very time considering the problem of conserving the land resources of the nation. It was said that dust filtered in around the doors and windows of the committee room in Washington where legislators were debating whether or not to establish the Soil Conservation Service. The following February the Soil Conservation and Domestic Allotment Act was passed, creating a new department of government to prevent such a loss of topsoil ever again, either by wind or by water. Shelter belts of trees were set out across the Great Plains. Cover crops were planted. Vast feats of engineering occurred on farms so that water would "walk, not run" downhill. All of it was done under a government program. (From *The Common Good,* Denver: National Farmers Union, 1978.)

WENDELL BERRY

In the past several days I have seen some of the worst-eroded corn fields that I have seen in this country in my life. This erosion is occurring on the cash-rented farms of farmers' widows and city farmers, absentee owners, the doctors and businessmen who buy a farm for the tax breaks or to have "a quiet place in the country" for the weekends. It is the direct result of economic and agricultural policy; it might be said to *be* an economic and agricultural policy. The signs of the "agridollar," big-business fantasy of the Butz mentality are all present: the absenteeism, the temporary and shallow interest of the land-renter, the row-cropping of slopes, the lack of rotation, the plowed-out waterways, the rows running up and down the hills. Looked at from the field's edge, this is ruin, criminal folly, moral idiocy. Looked at from Washington, D.C., from inside the "economy," it is called "free enterprise" and "full production." (From *The Unsettling of America.*)

WES JACKSON

It is well known that current dollar costs indicate little about the long-term costs to civilization. An economics which discounts the future is inherent in the environmental problem. Even so, the dollar costs to remove this "ecological capital" [soil] out of ditches, streams, rivers, reservoirs, harbors, lakes, and ponds is substantial. The Army Corps of Engineers worries about such phenomena as conveyance capacity of rivers, hindered navigation, and damage to Corps-constructed recreational marinas.

The U.S. Department of Agriculture has estimated that plant nutrient losses owing to erosion amount to around $18 billion per year in 1979 dollars. This is just to replace the nitrogen, phosphorus, and one-fourth of the potassium. To these higher production costs should be added the costs for degraded water and soil quality and, in some cases, the lowering of agricultural yields. The soil microflora, which assist in the breakdown of pesticides, are decreased as soil washes away. President Carter's message on the environment concluded that wind and water erosion "cause losses of organic matter important in the retention of soil moisture, the survival of soil microflora, and the chemical immobilization of toxic metals."

In forty-one years, from 1935 to 1976, our federal government has spent $20.7 billion "to conserve soil and water and to increase agricultural productivity." This cost includes "funding for cost-sharing, technical assistance, resource management, loans, research, and education." A sobering conclusion of the 1977 GAO report noted that the "recipients often did not fully implement suggested or required programs" and spent the money for production-oriented efforts. Follow-up by federal officials to encourage real soil conservation programs was practically nil.

One wonders how a great technological civilization such as ours would allow such atrocities to occur to the land and to the future. One is reminded of the Sumerians of Mesopotamia who invented the wheel six thousand years ago and whose mathematics we still employ in our clocks, which divide time into units of sixty. In one sense they were the best of peoples at their time, but in a resource conservation sense, they were the worst. Little grows over much of their old lands now. How about the enlightened Moses who led the Israelites to the Promised Land? It was "a good land, a land of brooks of water, of fountains and depths that spring out of the valleys and hills; a land of wheat and barley and vines and fig trees and pomegranates, a land of olive oil and honey; a land wherein thou shalt eat bread without scarceness; thou shalt not lack anything in it." Three thousand years later, bedrock is exposed throughout the uplands with the soil now in the narrow valleys or at the sea. Civilizations that are fountains of knowledge do not necessarily exercise wisdom.

One wonders whether a whimsical remark made many years ago by a U.S.D.A. soil scientist has taken on a profound truth. The scientist remarked that the ultimate goal of plant breeders and agronomists is "to grow forty bushels per acre of wheat on dry bedrock." (From *New Roots for Agriculture.*)

Land Appropriated for Development

VERNON CARSTENSEN

Thanks to the automobile, the hard-surfaced all-weather roads that have spread out from cities and towns (the invention of the gasoline tax in the early 1920s placed a tithe on all automobile gasoline; this provided a constant and growing harvest of money that made these roads possible), rural electrification, and a host of other related developments, the postwar years saw the once sharp edges of town and city become frayed and then disappear entirely in the urban sprawl. The sprawl has sometimes been light, sometimes heavy, as in Southern California where thousands upon thousands of acres of magnificent citrus groves and other farm lands have yielded to the outward march of the home builder, the tract developer, the shopping center. Great tollways and interstate superhighways have laced the land. Highway engineers, armed with almost limitless gas tax money and the right of eminent domain, have designed and built these great roads generally within the narrow imperatives of engineering values. If the road, with its landscaping, took all the arable land in a narrow, level, and fertile valley, or if it crippled a working farm by driving through its heart a great barrier of a superhighway, that was often of little concern. Engineering and design necessities were served and the farmer was paid for his land. (From "The Land of Plenty," in William T. Alderson, ed., *American Issues: Understanding Who We Are,* Nashville: American Association for State and Local History, 1976, pp. 17–31. Copyright © 1976 by the American Association for State and Local History.)

MINNESOTA CAMPAIGN LEAFLET

Alice Tripp's campaign grew out of the western Minnesota farmers' struggle against a high-voltage power line. . . .

The farmers found their land being taken away by an imperious and impersonal process that had no respect for their concerns. What truly surprised them was the role of their government. The utilities had planned the powerline; from the beginning the Governor and his agencies worked to help them build it.

State agencies turned a deaf ear to the farmers' legitimate concerns about need for the line, alternative routes, harm to an agricultural environment, and illegal practices. When the farmers convinced Pope County officials to refuse eminent domain rights to the utilities, the state Environmental Quality Board overruled them. The courts were no help. All they would consider was whether the agencies had followed the proper procedures.

The Governor called for a science court. When the farmers agreed, providing it consider the full range of concerns his agencies had swept under the rug, the Governor stopped talking about a science court. (From a leaflet, "Alice Tripp for Governor.")

TELEVISION DOCUMENTARY

The Kansas Power and Light Company has bought up almost 13,000 acres of land and is building here a mammoth energy center. When they were asked to sell their land, Alex Johnson and Delbert Pinick refused. The more he has learned about the power project, says Mr. Johnson, the more he is convinced that he made the morally right decision. Why, he wonders, did a power plant have to be built on some of the richest farmland in Kansas? Why is it necessary to erect on land like this one of the largest coal-burning operations in the world? Industry is the principal consumer of electric energy, and Kansas is dominantly agricultural, not industrial.

On a clear day, "could you still see forever," or would smog begin to cloud the horizon as tons of sulphur dioxide were discharged into the air year after year? What effect upon crops, even miles away, when the sulphur mixed with moisture in the air and fell back to earth as sulphuric acid, mixed with the rain? And why, wonders Alex Johnson, would 3,000 acres like this be flooded to form the cooling system for the energy center—a lake more than double the total land area of other plants generating almost the same amount of power? Had the company acquired ten times the amount of land it actually needed?

It had certainly acquired land that Alex Johnson needed. He owned himself only some 550 acres, but leased from absentee owners 2,200 acres in adjoining plots. A fourth of these he gave to wheat; on the rest he raised his cattle. But the absentee owners of Alex Johnson's leased lands have sold them to the power company and he, in turn, is being slowly forced to sell off his herd. For one who works the land and is in close communion with the earth, it is a sacred trust. For one who merely owns the land, well, land is land, and money is money.

When land is not cared for, man's ancient enemies take over, and in Kansas that means the thistle. The Power Center has not yet put to any use most of the acres it has bought—they have simply been removed from farm use. Thistle seeds have no respect for fences. They have blown over onto Alex Johnson's property, and are a menace to his remaining cattle. It took Alex and Betty Johnson fourteen years to build their farm, and they had hoped to give it to their sons—the dream of every farmer and his wife. For Alex and Betty Johnson that dream is almost at an end. But the dream did not die without a struggle—Alex Johnson and his neighbors consulted the Federal Power Commission, the Kansas Corporation Commission, the State Attorney General, and the Office of Environmental Health. The landowners eventually learned that there was not a federal or state agency that would question the need of Kansas Power and Light for such a large plant, or its right to condemn 13,000 acres of prime agricultural land.

Alex Johnson and his neighbors finally brought suit against the project—"taxpayers," in his words, "paying for court action to hold a public utility accountable to the public." The court decided against the farmers, and work on the project began—bulldozers and trucks now moving over land which had previously known only the tractor and the plow. Where before only grain silos had risen from the plains, four chimneys would now rise, each six hundred feet high. The huge plant was necessary, affirmed Kansas Power and Light, to meet the rising demand for electricity for both industrial and domestic use. This generating plant, in the words of the company, "will provide the electric energy necessary for the improvement of the quality of life Kansans are seeking and will serve the electric needs of over a million Kansans."

The energy complex will take at least ten years to complete—at a cost of almost one billion dollars—and the building of it will give employment to several hundred construction workers throughout that entire period. The operation of the plant itself will offer jobs to 250 people—twice the number of the farmers and their families who once lived and worked upon this land. All state and federal air quality standards will be met, pledges Kansas Power and Light, even when all four units are operating at capacity. Further, the company has selected low-sulphur coal from Wyoming precisely because it is best from an environmental point of view. Is the company then a public utility responsibly attempting to meet present and future energy demands, or is it, as Alex Johnson terms it, "an unbridled giant"?

Probably most would feel that Alex Johnson was wrong. But his question remains: how shall we best use our remaining land and water as we rush toward a future which will demand both more food and more energy? (From the transcript of a television documentary, "The Land," New York: National Broadcasting Company.)

ANITA PARLOW

For the past decade, North Carolina's mountains have endured the shock of rapid and uncontrolled development—development which is changing farming communities to "recreational shopping centers." Mountain and farmlands have been gobbled up and chopped away by developers who have transformed Watauga and Avery counties from farming valleys shielded by gently sloped mountains to a cacophony of strip-development fast-food chains. The land grab has boosted land prices so that farmers can't afford farmland and intruded a culture of affluence on farmers who are left to work as greenskeepers and domestics, commute to industry towns, or sell and move.

Developers say North Carolina farmers are simply following a national pattern of leaving the farms since World War II. But the national decrease in farm acreage harvested was 10 percent during the past decade, while the decrease in Avery County was nearly 40 percent. In more developed Watauga, it was a whopping 50 percent. Farmers admit that it's been getting more difficult to stay on the farm every year because of rising prices, but the financial blow caused by tourist resorts makes farm life almost impossible.

The seasonal beauty of the Blue Ridge and Appalachian chains attracted corporate developers, many of whom had already splattered the Florida coast with beachfront resorts. They saw a quick profit to be made in an area with four tourist seasons, low tax rates, accessibility to the Appalachian Development Highways, and a sixty-year history of exclusive, small resort communities. They came, they saw, they bought.

While the turnover of land to outsiders has been sizable, the boom was initiated locally, in the early sixties, by High Morton and the Robbins brothers, who recognized the profit to be made in major land development. Morton, called a "conservationist before the word was invented" by one of his salesmen, subdivided 7,000 acres of his family's land to create expensive and exclusive resort subdivisions. Morton's and the Robbins' developments would have 6,000 people living on delicate mountain land. The Robbins' Hound Ears development charges $20,000 for a half-acre lot with covenants to build $50,000 homes, and Morton's Invershield, a Scottish-deco community, costs $50,000 for two-acre lots and architectural covenants to build Scottish manor houses. The most exclusive and expensive development is Grandfather Mountain Golf and Country Club. Morton and Oklahoma oilman John Williams carved a suburban vacation complex into Grandfather Mountain and demanded $20,000 to $30,000 per acre, $6,500 for country club membership, $600 annual dues, and $80,000-to-$250,000 homes. (From *The Land Development Rag*, Knoxville: Southern Ministry in Higher Education, 1976.)

NORMAN COUSINS

Nothing would be more dangerous today to the human future than if the American standard were to be achieved in country after country. Consider what would happen if the present level of American industrialization, electrification, transportation, and consumption were extended to the rest of the world. A tidal wave of prosperity would sweep across the globe, but within a very few years the Earth would become uninhabitable. For it is not just affluence but the things that go with it that must be taken into account. If the American way of life were to be universalized, the world's atmosphere would have to sustain 200 times more sulphur dioxide and sulphur trioxide than it does now, 750 times more carbon monoxide, carbon dioxide, and benzopyrene, 10,000 times more asbestos. The streams, lakes, and oceans would be burdened with 175 times more chemical poisons. The Earth's forest areas would be reduced by two-thirds. Thirty million acres would be taken out of cultivation each year to make way for spreading cities and highways.

The total result would be the onset of another Ice Age. For

the massive increase of smoke and dust in the air would diminish sunlight and produce a significant lowering of the Earth's temperature. Even without respect to the cooling off of the Earth, an even greater danger would be the depletion of the world's oxygen supply caused by the chemical poisoning of the oceans and the consequent impairment of the process of photosynthesis.

What gives grim point to all this is that most of the world's nations, not excluding the Soviet Union and Communist China, are now resolutely bent on a program of intensive and massive industrialization as the best means of serving their peoples. Thus, whether with respect to the United States or other governments, there is little sense of global responsibility, little awareness of the need for planetary planning or of the fact that the most important questions and problems of our time are worldwide in scope, requiring a world philosophy to deal with them.

For years many Americans had no hesitation in prescribing their way of life as a comprehensive remedy for the ills of mankind. Terms such as "the American Century" or "the American Mission" reflected the conviction that we had created a design for living within the reach of all men who were ready to accept our institutions, and who were bold and ingenious enough to apply them. But now we must confront the stark fact that this design is contrary to the human interest.

The implications will of course be viewed differently by different people. Some Americans may find it difficult to adjust to the realization that the American dream no longer fits the generality of men. Some of them may feel that a freeze ought to be imposed on further development elsewhere, now that the adverse consequences of a high degree of industrialization are measurable in global terms. Other Americans, however, will recognize that the most useful thing we can do right now is not to try to shut everyone else off from the largesse we have enjoyed, but to bring our dominant energies to bear on the need to bring life into balance in our own land. What is required are not only new methods and programs for preventing and controlling pollution, but new ideas and values directed to a future made safe for man. In such a future, the good life would be measured more in terms of an improvement in human relationships than in any increase of the gross national product. Satisfactions would be reckoned more in terms of the full creative and moral development of the individual than in the pleasures made possible by generating vast quantities of electric power. There would be genuine joy in being able to draw a deep breath of clean air, scoop up a handful of rich loam, or put one's mouth to a cool brook. The restoration of the natural environment and the discovery of how to live at peace with it would become a national purpose. It is possible that the rest of the world would find this new purpose even more compelling and worthy of emulation than the present one.

Maybe this is what our young people are trying to tell us. (From "Needed: A New Dream," © June 20, 1970. *Saturday Review* Magazine. Reprinted by permission.)

Relationship to Nature

LEWIS THOMAS

We are told that the trouble with Modern Man is that he has been trying to detach himself from nature. He sits in the topmost tiers of polymer, glass, and steel, dangling his pulsing legs, surveying at a distance the writhing life of the planet. In this scenario, Man comes on as a stupendous lethal force, and the earth is pictured as something delicate, like rising bubbles at the surface of a country pond, or flights of fragile birds.

But it is illusion to think that there is anything fragile about the life of the earth; surely this is the toughest membrane imaginable in the universe, opaque to probability, impermeable to death. We are the delicate part, transient and vulnerable as cilia. Nor is it a new thing for man to invent an existence that he imagines to be above the rest of life; this has been his most consistent intellectual exertion down the millennia. As illusion, it has never worked out to his satisfaction in the past, any more than it does today. Man is embedded in nature.

The biologic science of recent years has been making this a more urgent fact of life. The new hard problem will be to cope with the dawning, intensifying realization of just how interlocked we are. The old, clung-to notions most of us have held about our special lordship are being deeply undermined. (From

The Lives of a Cell: Notes of a Biology Watcher, by Lewis Thomas. Copyright © 1971, 1972, 1973 by the Massachusetts Medical Society. Copyright © 1974 by Lewis Thomas. "The Lives of a Cell" was originally published in *The New England Journal of Medicine.* Reprinted by permission of Viking/Penguin, Inc.)

WENDELL BERRY

The most dangerous tendency in modern society, now rapidly emerging as a scientific-industrial ambition, is the tendency toward encapsulation of human order—the severance, once and for all, of the umbilical cord fastening us to the wilderness or the Creation. The threat is not only in the totalitarian desire for absolute control. It lies in the willingness to ignore an essential paradox: the natural forces that so threaten us are the same forces that preserve and renew us.

An enduring agriculture must never cease to consider and respect and preserve wildness. The farm can exist only within the wilderness of mystery and natural force. And if the farm is to last and remain in health, the wilderness must survive within the farm. That is what agricultural fertility is: the survival of natural process in the human order. To learn to preserve the fertility of the farm, Sir Albert Howard wrote, we must study the forest. (From *The Unsettling of America.*)

EMIL KARNIK

There used to be a lot of prairie chickens, yes. You got up in the morning, you could hear them "bobuling" in every direction from the place. Howling, just like a pigeon, you know. Mostly in the spring of the year. That's when they'd be on the hills, on the prairie. But God, you'd hear 'em bobuling.

Ducks! It was just like blackbirds in dose sloughs, just clouds and clouds of ducks. And geese and everyt'ing. Sometimes, in dose sloughs where the big geese had their nests, we'd take their eggs, and Mother would put them under hens, hatch 'em under the hens. And we had wild geese right to home. You tame dem. But they was flyers. They liked to fly away, and if they got away into the sloughs, with dem wild geese, dey was gone. And we didn't see 'em no more. Mother used to clip their wings, and then they'd grow up big enough, and then Mother used to butcher 'em. Didn't bother saving any at all. Because if we wanted any more, all we had to do was go hunt around the slough and pick up eggs and hatch our own.

Ducks, they used to be more of them than geese. Some sloughs, when they flew all up, it was just like a big flock of blackbirds. Clouds of ducks. (From Joe Paddock, ed., *The Things We Know Best: An Oral History of Olivia, Minnesota, and Its Surrounding Countryside*, Olivia, MN: Book 200, 1975.)

HENRY NASH SMITH

Although it was endlessly exciting for nineteenth-century Americans to contemplate the pioneer army moving westward at the command of destiny, and the Sons of Leatherstocking performing their improbable exploits in the wilderness, these themes had only an indirect bearing upon the major trends of economic and social development in American society. The forces which were to control the future did not originate in the picturesque Wild West beyond the agricultural frontier, but in the domesticated West that lay behind it.

With each surge of westward movement a new community came into being. These communities devoted themselves not to marching onward but to cultivating the earth. They plowed the virgin land and put in crops, and the great Interior Valley was transformed into a garden: for the imagination, the Garden of the World. The image of this vast and constantly growing agricultural society in the interior of the continent became one of the dominant symbols of nineteenth-century American society—a collective representation, a poetic idea (as Tocqueville noted in the early 1830s) that defined the promise of American life. The master symbol of the garden embraced a cluster of metaphors expressing fecundity, growth, increase, and blissful labor in the earth, all centering about the heroic figure of the idealized frontier farmer armed with that supreme agrarian weapon, the sacred plow. . . . The idea of the garden of the world . . . expressed the assumptions and aspirations of a whole society and the hint of narrative content supplied by the central figure of the Western farmer give it much of the character of a myth.

The myth of the garden affirmed that the dominant force in the future society of the Mississippi Valley would be agriculture. It is true that with the passage of time this symbol, like that of the Wild West, became in its turn a less and less accurate description of a society transformed by commerce and industry. When the new economic and technological forces, especially the power of steam working through river boats and locomotives, had done their work, the garden was no longer a garden. But the image of an agricultural paradise in the West, embodying group memories of an earlier, a simpler, and, it was believed, a happier state of society, long survived as a force in American thought and politics. So powerful and vivid was the image that down to the very end of the nineteenth century it continued to seem a representation, in Whitman's words, of the core of the nation, "the real genuine America." (Henry Nash Smith, *Virgin Land.* Cambridge: Harvard University Press, 1950.)

N. SCOTT MOMADAY

It is no doubt more difficult to imagine in 1970 the landscape of America than it was in, say, 1900. Our whole experience as a nation in this century has been a repudiation of the pastoral ideal which informs so much of the art and literature of the nineteenth century. One effect of the Technological Revolution has been to uproot us from the soil. We have become disoriented, I believe; we have suffered a kind of psychic dislocation of ourselves in time and space. We may be perfectly sure of where we are in relation to the supermarket and the next coffee break, but I doubt that any of us knows where he is in relation to the stars and to the solstices. Our sense of the natural order has become dull and unreliable. Like the wilderness itself, our sphere of instinct has diminished in proportion as we have failed to imagine truly what it is. And yet I believe that it is possible to formulate an ethical ideal of the land—a notion of what it is and must be in our daily lives—and I believe moreover that it is absolutely necessary to do so.

It would seem on the surface of things that a land ethic is something that is alien to, or at least dormant in, most Americans. Most of us in general have developed an attitude of indifference toward the land. (From "An American Land Ethic," in Self-Discovery through the Humanities, *Americans and the Land,* vol. 4, Washington, DC: National Council on the Aging, 1977.)

ALDO LEOPOLD

Conservation is a state of harmony between men and land. By land is meant all of the things on, over, or in the earth. Harmony with land is like harmony with a friend; you cannot cherish his right hand and chop off his left. That is to say, you cannot love game and hate predators; you cannot conserve the waters and waste the ranges; you cannot build the forest and mine the farm. The land is one organism. Its parts, like our own parts, compete with each other. The competitions are as much a part of the inner workings as the co-operations. You can regulate them—cautiously—but not abolish them.

The outstanding scientific discovery of the twentieth century is not television, or radio, but rather the complexity of the land organism. Only those who know the most about it can appreciate how little is known about it. The last word in ignorance is the man who says of an animal or plant: "What good is it?" If the land mechanism as a whole is good, then every part is good, whether we understand it or not. If the biota, in the course of aeons, has built something we like but do not understand, then who but a fool would discard seemingly useless parts? To keep every cog and wheel is the first precaution of intelligent tinkering. (From *A Sand County Almanac.*)

JEAN DORST

Conservation of nature implies conservation of natural resources as a whole, beginning with those of water, air, and, especially, soil, on which we depend for life. It also requires the protection of landscapes as a harmonious setting for man's life and his activities. All too often we have disfigured whole regions by poorly planned industrial units and agricultural projects. Man needs balance and beauty, and those who think they have no interest whatsoever in aesthetics are often much more sensitive to it than they realize.

We need to study these different problems today and to achieve a rational management of the earth's surface. Plans for development should ascertain for what purpose the land is best suited, and, especially in marginal zones, they should set aside large areas where natural habitats can be preserved. The old antagonism between the "protectors of nature" and the planners should cease. The former must learn that the survival of man requires intensive agriculture and a complete transformation of certain areas; they must abandon a number of sentimental prejudices, some of which have done serious harm to the cause they are defending.

On the other side, the technocrats must admit that man cannot free himself from certain biological laws, and that a rational exploitation of natural resources does not involve transforming habitats automatically and completely. They must understand that the preservation of natural areas constitutes land use quite as much as does their modification. A realistic agreement between economists and biologists can and must lead to reasonable solutions and assure the rational development of humanity in a setting in harmony with natural laws.

Those who deal with conservation often have a curiously guilty conscience. They seem to be apologizing for withdrawing certain areas of the globe from human influence and depriving man of a fair profit. They must abandon this attitude, for their opinions are quite as defensible as those of engineers charged with the transformation of a region. Like them, and with them, they must contribute to the total improvement of a territory, which implies maintaining some natural habitats in their original state. The preservation of rare species is only the best known of the multiple reasons for this.

We must, then, strike a balance between man and nature. To some people the term "natural balance" has a romantic connotation, but to biologists it is a realistic goal. They admit that man must transform part of the earth's surface for his own good, but they deny that he has the right to transform the entire surface of the world, since this would be against his own interest. Thus man will be the first to benefit from a reconciliation with nature. (From *Before Nature Dies* by Jean Dorst. Translated by Constance D. Sherman. Copyright © 1970 by William Collins Sons & Co., Ltd. Reprinted by permission of Houghton Mifflin Company.)

WES JACKSON

[Hugh Bennett in 1942 said:] "When you get out on the land with people, and work with them and talk with them about the productivity of the soil, there is some sort of common denominator there. I think that our statesmen, our educators, and all of our great men from the beginning of time have missed that point.

"When you begin to talk and work with the fertility of the soil and the way it relates to the welfare of humanity, you are talking a common language. It brings people closer together. It will bring nations closer together."

At the same meeting the international need was further articulated by Dr. John Detwiler, president of the Canadian Conservation Society. "We begin to realize," he began, "that an overcrowding of people on a diminished soil base may impinge on the intellect, lead to physical and nervous disorders, and break forth ultimately in the hidden hunger that brings on wars. Perhaps when we organize conservation on an international basis we can avoid the hidden hunger which brings on wars." In 1945, Detwiler sent a communication to the organ of the organization *The Land Quarterly*, which included, "To preach conservation at such a time, when all our resources, national and otherwise, are being sacrificed in unprecedented measure, might seem to some anomalous, even ironical. . . . But we firmly believe, and now are more acutely aware than ever, that conservation is basically related to the peace of the world and the future of the race." The Journal carried an "Other Lands" section as further indication of the group's awareness of the connection between prosperous soil and peaceful people. (From *New Roots for Agriculture.*)

SUSAN GRIFFIN

Only now, we name ourselves. Only now, as we think of ourselves as passing, do we utter the syllables. Do we list all that we are. That we know in ourselves. We know ourselves to be made from this earth. We know this earth is made from our bodies. For we see ourselves. And we are nature. Nature weeping. Nature speaking of nature to nature. The red-winged blackbird flies in us, in our inner sight. We see the arc of her flight. We measure the ellipse. We predict its climax. We are amazed. We are moved. We fly. . . .

. . . When I let this bird fly to her own purpose, when this bird flies in the path of her own will, the light from this bird enters my body, and when I see the beautiful arc of her flight, I love this bird, when I see the arc of her flight, I fly with her, enter her with my mind, leave myself, die for an instant, live in the body of this bird whom I cannot live without, as part of the body of the bird will enter my daughter's body, because I know I am made from this earth, as my mother's hands were made from this earth, as her dreams came from this earth, and all that I know, I know in this earth, the body of the bird, this pen, this paper, these hands, this tongue speaking, all that I know speaks to me through this earth and I long to tell you, you who are earth too, and listen as we speak to each other of what we know: the light is in us. (From *Woman and Nature*, New York: Harper & Row, 1980.)

LEWIS THOMAS

Statistically, the probability of any one of us being here is so small that you'd think the mere fact of existing would keep us all in a contented dazzlement of surprise. We are alive against the stupendous odds of genetics, infinitely outnumbered by all the alternates who might, except for luck, be in our places.

Even more astounding is our statistical improbability in physical terms. The normal, predictable state of matter throughout the universe is randomness, a relaxed sort of equilibrium, with atoms and their particles scattered around in an amorphous muddle. We, in brilliant contrast, are completely organized structures, squirming with information at every covalent bond. We make our living by catching electrons at the moment of their excitement by solar photons, swiping the energy released at the instant of each jump and storing it up in intricate loops for ourselves. We violate probability, by our nature. To be able to do this systematically, and in such wild varieties of form from viruses to whales, is extremely unlikely; to have sustained the effort successfully for the several billion years of our existence, without drifting back into randomness, was nearly a mathematical impossibility.

Add to this the biological improbability that makes each member of our own species unique. Everyone is one in three billion at the moment, which describes the odds. Each of us is a self-contained, freestanding individual, labeled by specific protein configurations at the surfaces of cells, identifiable by whorls of fingertip skin, maybe even by special medleys of fragrance. You'd think we'd never stop dancing. (From *The Lives of a Cell*.)

WALT WHITMAN

I swear the earth shall surely be complete to him or her who
shall be complete,
The earth remains jagged and broken only to him or her who
remains jagged and broken.
I swear there is no greatness or power that does not emulate
those of the earth,
There can be no theory of any account unless it corroborate the
theory of the earth,
No politics, song, religion, behavior, or what not, is of account,
unless it compare with the amplitude of the earth.
Unless it face the exactness, vitality, impartiality, rectitude of
the earth.

(From "A Song of the Rolling Earth," Walt Whitman, *Poetry and Prose.* New York: The Library of America, 1982.)

Stewardship

WENDELL BERRY

In order to understand our own time and predicament and the work that is to be done, we would do well to . . . say that we are divided between exploitation and nurture. . . .

Let me outline as briefly as I can what seem to me the characteristics of these opposite kinds of mind. I conceive a strip-miner to be a model exploiter, and as a model nurturer I take the old-fashioned idea or ideal of a farmer. The exploiter is a specialist, an expert; the nurturer is not. The standard of the exploiter is efficiency; the standard of the nurturer is care. The exploiter's goal is money, profit; the nurturer's goal is health—his land's health, his own, his family's, his community's, his country's. Whereas the exploiter asks of a piece of land only how much and how quickly it can be made to produce, the nurturer asks a question that is much more complex and difficult: What is its carrying capacity? (That is: How much can be taken from it without diminishing it? What can it produce *dependably* for an indefinite time?) The exploiter wishes to earn as much as possible by as little work as possible; the nurturer expects, certainly, to have a decent living from his work, but his characteristic wish is to work as well as possible. The competence of the exploiter is in organization; that of the nurturer is in order—a human order, that is, that accommodates itself both to other order and to mystery. The exploiter typically serves an institution or organization; the nurturer serves land, household, community, place. The exploiter thinks in terms of numbers, quantities, "hard facts"; the nurturer in terms of character, condition, quality, kind. (From *The Unsettling of America.*)

ALDO LEOPOLD

The "key-log" which must be moved to release the evolutionary process for an ethic is simply this: quit thinking about decent land use as solely an economic problem. Examine each question in terms of what is ethically and esthetically right, as well as what is economically expedient. A thing is right when it tends to preserve the integrity, stability, and beauty of the biotic community. It is wrong when it tends otherwise.

It of course goes without saying that economic feasibility limits the tether of what can or cannot be done for the land. It always has and it always will. The fallacy the economic determinists have tied around our collective neck, and which we now need to cast off, is the belief that economics determines *all* land use. This is simply not true. An innumerable host of actions and attitudes, comprising perhaps the bulk of all land relations, is determined by the land-user's tastes and predilections, rather than by his purse. The bulk of all land relations hinge on investments of time, forethought, skill, and faith rather than on investments of cash. As a land-user thinketh, so is he.

A land ethic . . . reflects the existence of an ecological conscience, and this in turn reflects a conviction of individual responsibility for the health of the land. Health is the capacity of the land for self-renewal. Conservation is our effort to understand and preserve this capacity. (From *A Sand County Almanac.*)

WENDELL BERRY

We have been wrong to believe that competition invariably results in the triumph of the best. Divided body and soul, man and woman, producer and consumer, nature and technology, city and country are thrown into competition with one another. And none of these competitions is ever resolved in the triumph of one competitor, but only in the exhaustion of both. (From *The Unsettling of America.*)

ELIZABETH DODSON GRAY

The covenant in creation has never been properly understood. Instead, the covenant has always been construed as something apart from creation. Even though the Genesis myth pronounced the goodness of all of creation, Judeo-Christian religion never saw that in the creation of the world there had been a covenant given. . . .

What had been completely overlooked was that God long ago had made a fundamental, initial, and sustaining covenant with all of creation. Through the millennia God has been continually loyal to this covenant with an ongoing renewal of the seasons, the generations, and of creation itself. Because we missed seeing all that, we have not seen "honoring creation" as our side of the covenant. . . .

We must re-myth our world! Lewis Mumford has observed that humanity dreams itself into existence. Our old dream has become a nightmare; we must dream a better dream. Perhaps . . . we will see a new vision, a vision of the Garden revisited, without the old oppressive patriarchal stories. It is a vision of harmony, of wholeness. It is a vision of diversity and interconnection. It is a vision of human life—from the cell to the household to the whole human society—caught up in a symbiotic dance of cosmic energy and sensual beauty, throbbed by a rhythm that is greater than our own, which births us into being and decays us into dying, yet whose gifts of life are incredibly good though mortal and fleeting.

Perhaps what we need to do is to turn the Genesis myth upon its head. Perhaps this finite planet and the here-and-now is our Eden. . . .

Perhaps the limits of our finite planet are like the biblical angel with the flaming sword, ready to cast into outer darkness those unable to perceive and live within the mixed blessings of the creation that God has prepared equally for all species, all sexes, all races, all classes. Perhaps our appropriate aspiration is not "dominion" but "praise!" (From *Green Paradise Lost: Re-Mything Genesis*, Wellesley, MA: Roundtable Press, 1979.)

WENDELL BERRY

For our healing we have on our side one great force: the power of Creation, with good care, with kindly use, to heal itself. (From *The Unsettling of America.*)

THOMAS F. HORNBEIN

From the beginning we had seen virtually no wilderness. Rice terraces had climbed thousands of feet up hillsides, prayer flags flapped at the passes; paths occasionally edged with mani walls crisscrossed the country. For all the size, for all the intransigent power of the ice-crusted wall to the north, wilderness, as western man defines it, did not exist. Yet there was no impression of nature tamed. It seemed to me that here man lived in continuous harmony with the land, as much and as briefly a part of it as all its other occupants. He used the earth with gratitude, knowing that care was required for continued sustenance. He rotated crops, controlled the cutting of wood, bulwarked his fields against erosion. In this peaceful coexistence, man was the invited guest. (From *Everest: The West Ridge* by Thomas F. Hornbein. Copyright 1965 by the Sierra Club. Reprinted by permission of Sierra Club Books.)

E. E. SCHUMACHER

Let us ask then: How does work relate to the end and purpose of man's being? It has been recognized in all authentic teachings of mankind that every human being born into this world has to work not merely to keep himself alive but to strive toward perfection. To keep himself alive, he needs various goods and services, which will not be forthcoming without human labor. To perfect himself, he needs purposeful activity in accordance with the injunction: "Whichever gift each of you have received, use it in service to one another, like good stewards dispensing the grace of God in its varied forms." From this, we may derive the three purposes of human work as follows:

First, to provide necessary and useful goods and services.

Second, to enable every one of us to use and thereby perfect our gifts like good stewards.

Third, to do so in service to, and in cooperation with, others, so as to liberate ourselves from our inborn egocentricity.

This threefold function makes work so central to human life that it is truly impossible to conceive of life at the human level without work. "Without work, all life goes rotten," said Albert Camus, "but when work is soulless, life stifles and dies." (From *Good Work*, New York: Harper & Row, 1979.)

MARGE PIERCY

The people I love best
jump into work head first
without dallying in the shallows
and swim off with sure strokes almost out of sight.
They seem to become natives of that element,
the black sleek heads of seals
bouncing like half-submerged balls.

I love people who harness themselves, an ox to a heavy
  cart,
who pull like water buffalo, with massive patience,
who strain in the mud and the muck to move things
  forward,
who do what has to be done, again and again.

I want to be with people who submerge
in the task, who go into the fields to harvest
and work in a row and pass the bags along,
who stand in the line and haul in their places,
who are not parlor generals and field deserters
but move in a common rhythm
when the food must come in or the fire be put out.

The work of the world is common as mud.
Botched, it smears the hands, crumbles to dust.
But the thing worth doing well done
has a shape that satisfies, clean and evident.
Greek amphoras for wine or oil,
Hopi vases that held corn, are put in museums
but you know they were made to be used.
The pitcher cries for water to carry
and a person for work that is real.

(From *Circles on the Water: Selected Poems of Marge Piercy*, by Marge Piercy. Copyright 1973 by Marge Piercy. Reprinted by permission of Alfred A. Knopf, Inc.)

WENDELL BERRY

To enrich the earth I have sowed clover and grass
to grow and die. I have plowed in the seeds
of winter grains and of various legumes,
their growth to be plowed in to enrich the earth.

I have stirred into the ground the offal
and the decay of the growth of past seasons
and so mended the earth and made its yield increase.
All this serves the dark. Against the shadow
of veiled possibility my workdays stand
in a most asking light. I am slowing falling
into the fund of things. And yet to serve the earth,
not knowing what I serve, gives a wideness
and a delight to the air, and my days
do not wholly pass. It is the mind's service
for when the will fails so do the hands
and one lives at the expense of life.
After death, willing or not, the body serves,
entering the earth. And so what was heaviest
and most mute is at last raised up into song.

WES JACKSON

We "civilized people" are a bit better about thinking of our future needs, but we may already have absorbed most of our foresight. During most of our conscious hours even now, we simply take (as we always have) from the environment, without much thought. This pattern of behavior is likely very deep within us and may not be mitigated without internalized pressure from a very strong ethic. Before the fall through agriculture, when our numbers were few, our tools simple, when we were altogether limited in our destructive ability, like the Bushmen, such an ethic was unnecessary.

One of our main troubles, now that our species is out of its natural context, is that we oversimplify our problems and misidentify their roots. The proposed solutions which come pouring forth are not matched to the subtle intricacies of the problem. For example, William Tucker, writing in the *Atlantic Monthly,* suggested that the solution to the erosion of our soils may lie in a revival of organic farming techniques. These techniques did not, of course, save the soils before 1940. But that is a lateral point. He praised the organic farmer, but in a final paragraph he asked if there "are enough people in the country willing to give the time and attention to the soil that is required by organic farming." The tough-minded producer may reply that we just have to develop the discipline and "shape up." People born in sin, his unconscious may say, are born undeserving and must exercise the necessary discipline.

The born-in-innocence approach, on the other hand, remembers that nature took good care of us for millions of years before we assumed such a huge role in food production. Since our assumption of more of the burden has steadily undercut nature's chances to provide on a sustainable basis (even though total production on a per acre basis is many times greater), let us look to her again for some clues, for some standard against which we can judge our agricultural practices. If we assume this latter, and I hope more enlightened, myth, isn't it likely we will find ourselves involved in more harmonious agricultural patterns and fewer patterns of destruction? If we make this agriculture less human-dependent and more self-renewing, then the new agriculture, based more on the principles of nature, can afford us a greater opportunity to take without thought for the morrow and still be sustained. As we look to a new agriculture, we cannot, nor should we, separate our agriculture from our religion or from our ethics. All these are most life-enhancing when they are an inseparable one. So as we move toward a sustainable agriculture, we will necessarily develop an ethic with sustainability at its core. (From *New Roots for Agriculture.*)

PAUL WILLIAMS

Homo sap, that creature who believes his purpose is to control and conquer Nature, is just now beginning to remember the obvious—that he is a part of Nature himself.

He has fought his way to the top of the planetary spinal cord, inflicting damage every step of the way. Now, bewildered, he looks around: *What am I doing here?*

Assuming responsibility, answers a still, small voice all around him.

(From *Das Energi,* New York: Warner Books, 1973.)

· III ·

Whole Vision

·13·

Food Production in the New Paradigm

UNTIL very recently, the future of agriculture in the United States has been envisioned in straight-line ascent from present-day realities. By the turn of the century, presumably, there would be perhaps no more than one hundred thousand superfarms, owned by individual families or corporations, providing food and fiber for all the rest of us. These farms of many thousands of acres would be highly technological, their soil tilled perhaps by microwaves, their crops protected from the elements by plastic coverings. These crops would be made up of plants genetically engineered to draw nitrogen fertilizer from the air, to resist frost, be tolerant of salt water, and so on, ad infinitum.

This, then, is the future for which our agricultural establishment is planning. Most men and women of this persuasion would find it hard to imagine any other possibility. It seems, however, that the more we focus on a single strategy for doing things, the more clearly we see the flaws in that strategy. Overwhelmed by the social and environmental costs of our present agricultural productivity, many of our visionaries are now imagining a different approach to the future. These men and women may well be on the verge of an evolutionary shift in human consciousness that seems to be a shift in paradigm or framework. That is, the mental framework through which we view the world is changing at a very fundamental level. Change this framework through which we release our energies, and everything thereafter will be altered in accord with the structure of the new framework.

Among many futurists, environmentalists, and New Age thinkers, the idea of the paradigm shift has lost its vogue. Some are simply tired of hearing about it. Others, because the concept implies that the shift is more or less inevitable, regard the concept as dangerous. It is their belief that such a shift will be accomplished only through dedication and hard work, and that we must not be lulled by any suggestion of inevitability. It is my belief that the truth may lie somewhere in between. Commitment and effort are, of course, absolutely essential, but, as I argue more fully below, it is the discomfort inherent in our problems themselves that underlies our commitment and effort and forces us to change. That is, pain produces change. In any case, we must develop a clear idea of our preferred future, and for that reason, if no other, we should explore the "new paradigm" as it might express itself in the agriculture of the future.

Paradigm shifts are nothing new in the history of the human race. Historians of philosophy identify the periods in which specific paradigms dominated us as the Age of Enlightenment, the Age of Reason, and so forth. Many believe that we are now in the early stages of a very large and comprehensive shift. As always, the energy behind it has arisen from the discomfort, the dis-ease, created by the aging of the previous paradigm. The cultural and environmental imbalances created by doing things in one way for a very long time have now come to the fore, and problems have begun to crowd in from all sides.

A cultural shift such as we are describing is equivalent to the passages through which individual humans must suffer at various stages of life, and may be considered part of our collective growth process. The old paradigm is not necessarily bad, but it is no longer appropriate to circumstances as they have evolved. The shift (having to learn to "act our age") may often be painful, a sort of initiation process for the entire human race. As with the individual human, we too may collectively balk at such change. Or we may not understand what is expected of us and thereby fail to move on to the next level of healthy maturity. It is extremely important, therefore, to create a clear vision of the desired future.

On its most simple level the present paradigm shift might be described as a movement away from the machine as the model by which we understand the workings of the universe and toward the interconnected ecosystem. On a deeper and more complex level, Fritjof Capra, in his book *The Turning Point,* has described this shift in the Oriental terminology of yin and yang. We are now moving, it would seem, in a yin direction. Away, say, from the masculine and toward the feminine. Away from linear, rational, mechanistic approaches; toward more holistic, feeling, and intuitive approaches. Though the balancing of yin and yang is apparent in *all* phenomena, the following are emphases within the overall swing—should it in fact be occurring—that we believe will especially influence the ways in which food will be produced in the future:

1. From a fascination with the machine or factory to the interconnected ecosystem as our primary model for both understanding and acting in the world;
2. From a materialistic to a more spiritual approach to life;
3. From a competitive to a more cooperative relationship to the world around us;
4. From a focus on the individual as the center of our affairs to a focus on the community;
5. From a belief in maximizing the size of our enterprises to a belief in finding the appropriate size for them;
6. From centralized control of our enterprises to decentralization;
7. From highly concentrated urban populations to larger rural populations.

These shifts have been listed as if they were independent, but they tend to be fully interconnected, one with the other, a seamless web. If the new system of agriculture is to be harmoniously balanced, healthy, it is unlikely that one of these shifts could occur independently of the others. We will shortly look into what these particular shifts might mean to food production, but first it will be useful to consider briefly our current approach to agriculture.

Modern production agriculture is a quite matured expression of the old paradigm factory-model. Ian R. Manners, in his essay

"Agricultural Activities and Environmental Stress," provides an accurate picture of this current approach to farming:

> Modern agricultural systems remain dependent on the soil as a medium in which to retain roots, water, and nutrients and to expose plants to the sun, but in every other respect they can be regarded as artificial ecosystems that function only as a result of extensive human manipulation. Commercial seed preparation and chemical pesticides have replaced natural controls on population numbers in an attempt to remove weeds and to reduce competition from insect pests; and genetic manipulation has replaced natural processes of plant evolution and selection. Even the decomposing element has been altered, for plant growth is harvested and soil fertility is maintained, not through the natural recycling of nutrients, but through the application of commercial fertilizers.[1]

Though production in this country remains high—due in part to our tremendous, though diminishing, resource in land—social, economic, and environmental problems have been increasing at a rapid rate. A successful new framework for thought must contain the potential solutions to these problems. If new paradigm thinking is correct, our future success and fulfillment in agriculture, as elsewhere, will increasingly be tied to our ability to express the eco-model of interconnectedness in the ways in which we relate to nature and society. In one way or another, all other aspects of the paradigm shift listed previously are contained within this model. Let's look more closely, then, at these other shifts to see how they might affect food production in the future.

First, there is the projected swing from a materialistic to a more spiritual perspective. Over the past two decades, a shift of this nature has clearly begun in the United States. We have seen it in a renewal of the established denominations of Christianity, in the formation of cults, in intense interest in Eastern religions, in a burgeoning consciousness movement—it is everywhere. To the degree that this shift is authentic, our values, our perception of "the good," will in time shift in accordance. For one thing, if this religious renewal is truly spiritual, accumulation of material goods, beyond reasonable need, should become less important to us.

Any prediction of a shift away from materialism is likely to be met with cynicism. At present, materialism and Christianity are loving bedfellows. And many spiritually oriented New Age thinkers now hold forth on prosperity consciousness. It can be argued, however, that more and more people are in fact looking to philosophies of voluntary simplicity often even in a "selfish" effort to avoid the rat race. Many others, though not necessarily courting simpliciy, are choosing not to maximize their earning potential so that they can enjoy experiential values such as travel and living close to nature. Should problems inherent in the decaying paradigm become increasingly burdensome, such alternatives will presumably become attractive to a larger and larger segment of our population. In *The Turning Point,* Capra describes our current concentration on profit and production as the last hurrah of conservative materialism, through which the new paradigm will rise like the green grass of spring.

Should this shift occur, excess accumulation, like excess fat on the human body, will be disparaged, will be considered "stolen" from the larger wholes of society, nature, and the future. Our status in society will be tied to the grace with which we live in voluntary simplicity. Whatever this would mean to our economy, there would clearly be far less stress on our ecosystems—and perhaps on ourselves. Food, of course, enough high-quality food, would remain one of those indispensables toward which we could turn full human attention.

In part, such a shift toward the spiritual would find focus in an effort to develop our highest human potential. As so many people of vision are now doing, humanity in general would increasingly strive toward great stress-free physical health, lively and creative minds, and a consciousness which through prayer and meditation, among other things, would be ever growing toward that mystical awareness of our being one with the larger whole.

As an extension of, indeed inseparable from, great personal health, the health and harmony of the whole(s) will become a primary human concern. The health and well-being of farmland—of which our food and, finally, we ourselves are an extension—will be an absolute in our holistic and spiritual caring for the world.

Many believe that at some point in the history of humankind a light went out of our lives. It would be the point at which we left the "garden," which is equated with our hunting and gathering period, and began our struggle to subdue nature. Our belief that the earth and its life (other than human) are no longer sacred has given us great power over them. In chapter four, we quoted the Nez Percé Smohalla to show how restrictive a deeply sacred relationship with the land can be: "You ask me to cut grass and make hay and sell it and be rich like white men. But how dare I cut off my mother's hair?"[2] Such belief and love imposed great limitations on what traditional cultures could do in the world, but, as a result of denying the sacred life of Earth, European culture has done far-reaching harm to it. And some light has indeed gone out of our lives.

As we come once again to embrace the sacredness of creation, it will occur to us that the food we eat is also sacred—especially if it becomes other than cheap and abundant. It is my understanding that traditional cultures have seen food as a sacred cord, an umbilicus, that tied them to the rest of creation. This is apparent in the ritualized prayers that were (and are) part and parcel with the hunt, the harvest, and the meal. Food is one of the ways in which nature, the creation, flows through us. In our efforts to develop our full potential, new paradigm thinking suggests we will eat more carefully to enhance the health of our bodies and the clarity of our thought. In so doing it will become even more clear to us what a debt we owe the larger whole.

The heightened consciousness that could be expected to accompany the spiritual shift we have been describing would lead, proponents argue, to mindfulness in the things we do. Work, when expressed from such consciousness, is done with concentration and care. There is no avoidance. Word is done to the hilt. In such doing, the argument goes, we find freedom, and what we accomplish is substantial and worthy of a sacred place.

In this context, it is interesting to note that the Chinese, following their revolution, doubled their agricultural production with essentially no change in technology. Attached as we are to factory-model production, it is hard for us to imagine that the food needs of our modern world could be met in any other way. Yet China and other "underdeveloped" nations produce far more food per acre than we do. As is well known, China is now self-sufficient in food production, has even recently become an exporter of food. It feeds its one billion people (a quarter of the world's population) on a less favorable land base than our own. Former Secretary of Agriculture Bob Bergland, in fact, stated that the Chinese may produce as much as nine times per acre what we do in the United States.[3]

Great mindfulness, too, will see ever more deeply into the effects of our actions on the interconnected whole, the ecosystem. A farmer or gardener who identifies with the ecosystem as an extension of him- or herself may, for example, be trusted to decide when, if ever, an application of pesticide is needed for the long-term well-being of the greater garden.

Such mindfulness is sensitive to the fact that human food production is not, at heart, a struggle *against* the forces of creation, but is an allowing of these forces, with our cautious guidance and occasional intrusion, to express themselves as fully as possible in our food plants. Something such as this, it would seem, would be the definition of agriculture when heightened mind looks at food production through the framework of the eco-model.

The paradigm shift will also take us away from intensely competitive values toward more cooperative ones. No one in the United States is unaffected by arguments in support of a competitive value system. The values of our business community and even our schools are in large part premised on competition. And contemporary agriculture, in many ways still adhering to a frontier values system, continues to see itself in competition with the land. Half of our topsoil is gone, but we still hold to the competitive edge we have established. Again and again, with minor variations, we hear, "We must not take from the farmer the right to do what he wants with his own land." But our frontier period is over. The land has been subdued. For its well-being and our own we must now learn to cooperate with it.

Looking to the model of the interconnected ecosystem, it is clear that the overall well-being of the ecosystem is one enormously important reason for the competition within it. Predator-prey competitions, for instance, create good health for both at the species level. Competition that enhances the well-being of the individual must always take place within a larger context of cooperation. If any one component of the system, in an effort to maximize itself, becomes too successful, the entire system gets out of balance; the entire system suffers, even to the point of extinction for the offending portion, if not the system itself. Competition among farmers—who have for the most part expressed the competitive and materialistic values of the old paradigm—has in the past fifty years killed off nearly 80 percent of all U.S. farms, and the toll is now mounting at an accelerating rate.

As an example of a more cooperative approach within the food industry, urban food co-ops have attempted to transcend narrow self-interest and deal with problems of both the producer and the consumer. They offer, in certain areas of the country, an interesting alternative to the competitive supermarket approach. They provide whole foods, often locally and organically grown. Packaging is kept to a minimum. Customers often weigh their own purchases. Collectively managed, they are staffed by volunteers who receive for their efforts a substantial reduction in the cost of their food.

The shift from competition to cooperation will also be seen in a change in focus from the individual to the community. When I collect oral history from rural old-timers, I ask what they miss most about the past. Again and again I hear that it is the spirit of neighborhood and community: "everyone helping everyone else," working and playing together in all the activities of their lives. Those community traditions and rituals of interconnectedness ran deep, back into the Middle Ages and beyond. In truth, they were an actual expression of the ecosystem—they rose with us from it and can revive with it.

The way in which our first immigrants spaced their dwellings and, thereby, their lives may have been a mistake. There was a great wealth of land, and each family wanted its own domain. This spacing led to unconnectedness, a loneliness that even the automobile and TV have not fully erased. As depicted, for instance, in the life of Beret in Ole Rolvaag's novel *Giants in the Earth,* this isolation was often hardest on women, sometimes leading even to madness.

On this same land Native Americans had lived in closely knit tribal groups. And back in Europe, where land holdings were much smaller, people also usually lived in small villages. Farmers worked surrounding fields and returned to their community at night. There was no hope, in such a system, of achieving great personal wealth. No hope, as had Per Hansa, Beret's husband in *Giants in the Earth,* of owning more land than "many a king of old," but there was, in compensation, that rest within the harmoniously interconnected whole to which we belong. A rest for which many search aimlessly today. Once sprung from the restraints of the overall system, we find no respite along the tangled pathways of personal desire.

In his book *Darkness and Scattered Light,* William Irwin Thompson describes what he calls the metaindustrial village. He believes such villages will be the most basic social unit in the coming system. They will be, at once, social centers, factories, universities, and centers for food production. Their design will reflect this diversity of function. When these villages reach their maturity, they will express humanity's four major human economies: hunting and gathering, agriculture, industry, and cybernetics.

Thompson believes the people of these villages will be contemplative in nature, tuned in through meditation and other technologies of the sacred to the wisdom of the cosmos. At the same time, through miniaturization of technology, these villages will also be universities, in immediate and continuing electronic contact with the learning resources of the planet. The metaindustrial village will be the laboratory of the ongoing human race, as it makes its adjustments to harmonize itself within the greater whole. "If there is not a complex informational flow which relates the village to the planet, then you do not have a metaindustrial village, but simply a regressive hippie commune."[4]

Miniaturization of technology, while allowing the village to take on the function of a university, will also help it to transcend the sense of isolation and parochialism that many believe have plagued our rural food-producing populations. It has long been a dream of humanity to link a life in nature with something of the cultural richness possible in the urban setting. New paradigm thinkers argue also that the move away from the materialism and the severe work ethic that have so characterized our rural communities will be a tremendous boon to village life as well. As Gary Snyder has reminded us, referring to rituals, a great part of traditional village life has been participation in the "opera" and the "ballet."

It may be that the new paradigm will support those who believe the whole concept of individual ownership of land to be a profane one. Most of rural America retains its roots in the Christian church, and the Bible is quite clear that human ownership of land is a very tenuous designation: "You are only strangers and guests."

From the sacred point of view, assuming the reasonable well-being of the individual, private ownership of land is justified only insofar as it serves the well-being of the greater whole. Nevertheless, idealists in the United States have heretofore tended to hold out for many small landowners. The argument, most often attributed to Thomas Jefferson, is that these many small and independent landholders will create a broad base of free people for a democracy. However, public policy, private business practice, and individual greed have all worked in the interim to squeeze small farmers from their holdings. As mentioned before, since the 1930s we have lost nearly 80 percent of our farms.

Our approach to ownership of land often astonished the Native Americans. They were shocked that individuals could buy and sell parcels of nature and then go about changing them almost beyond recognition—over hundreds of thousands of square miles. "It was incomprehensible to the Indian that one person should have exclusive possession of parts of the earth. The warrior chief, Tecumseh, reacted with astonishment to the demands of white buyers: 'Sell the country. . . ? Why not sell the air, the clouds, the great sea?' "[5]

For Native Americans "ownership" was a tribal matter. The village commons of preindustrial Europe was, it seems, a similar use of land. And the community land trust approach to ownership, as experimented with at the Featherfield Farm Project in southwest Georgia, is also similar to the tribal approach of Native Americans:

> The community land trust is a legal entity, a quasi-public body, chartered to hold land in stewardship for all mankind present and future while protecting the legitimate use-rights of its residents.
>
> The community land trust is *not* primarily concerned with *common ownership.* Rather, its concern is

> for *ownership for the common good,* which may or may not be combined with common ownership.
>
> Land is held by the community land trust in perpetuity—probably never to be sold. Thus, the problems of exchange are virtually eliminated. The trust leases the land to the users with the expectation of preserving or enhancing its long-range resource value. The leases are long-term, restricted to the actual users of the land; absentee control and subleasing are specifically proscribed. The residents have secure use rights to the land and are free to control and build their own community through cooperative organizations or individual homesteads.[6]

The concept here, then, has moved from that of property to *trusterty.* The trusterty approach to ownership would seem to be in harmony with the new paradigm model. For those who now own land this might seem a terrible loss. For those many would-be farmers, on the other hand, who see little hope of ever owning their own land, such an opportunity might seem a dream come true.

Currently in the United States the forces of competitive, factory-model farming are causing the ownership of farmland to be concentrated in the hands of fewer and fewer people. Many surviving farmers are overextended, threatened by liquidations and foreclosures, on the one hand, and high stress, ulcers, heart disease, mental illness, murder and suicide on the other. The original unharmonious component, very large farms, has invaded the whole system, creating dis-ease on all levels.

In the coming generation we may have a very small landed class. One can question the wisdom of allowing the greatest concentration of prime farmland in the world to be controlled by a tiny handful of people or corporations. Looked at through the eco-model, such great concentrations may create dangerous blockage (of the flow of natural wealth) in the "circulatory system" of the agricultural body and the greater social body.

What is to be sought, then, is the *optimum* size for the given bio-region, *optimum* size for the given style of food culture, *optimum* size for the given neighborhood and community. A key to wise decision making, in all areas of the new agriculture, will be to balance each component in relation to the overall system. The individual farmer, in accepting this balance, may be sacrificing the euphoria that comes with outdoing one's neighbors. Instead, however, he or she will enjoy living in a harmonious system that increasingly can be seen as not other than ourselves.

Should the new paradigm take hold, then, we can expect a reversal of the current trend toward giantism: food culture will take place in increasingly smaller units. Victor Ray, whose thinking we have often turned to in this book, once told an American Farm Project gathering the story of a man who intended to send several children to college on the earnings from his forty-acre farm. When questioned about this, the man replied, "If I can't do it on forty, I'll do it on twenty."

This story, of course, expresses the belief that, in contrast to our current philosophy, more can be accomplished through diversity and intensification of effort than through expansion with its dependence on expensive technology and chemicals.

New paradigm farms will use the forms of energy expressed most directly and conveniently within their ecosystems, the various forms of solar energy. Forecasters with a more technical bias speak not of the new paradigm, but of the coming Solar Age. Many approaches, such as wind and water flow, are old, even ancient. Others—the solar collector and the methane generator—are more recent. An alternative science and technology have been steadily evolving to make solar energy more efficient. Should "greed" shift somewhat, away from self-interest (technology you can put a meter on) to interest in the well-being of the whole, this evolution in soft technology may well move forward at an exponential rate. In any case, the diffuse nature of solar energy is yet another basis for the expectation of ever smaller and more diverse approaches to agriculture in the future.

In this new era, the most important question of all, when we consider the optimum size of a farm, just may be the optimum *human* arrangement. Where do we truly come into synchrony with the whole? In what circumstances does our soul find rest? Will this be the pastoral mixed farm of the turn of the century? Or, perhaps, a garden?

Modern agriculture has been amazingly successful at transforming the land to fit its monocultural factory model. Once accomplished, control from distant power centers was relatively easy. Absentee ownership has, in fact, been a major cause of bad soil stewardship. In the new agriculture, land will be farmed according to its most individual characteristics. Since food production systems will be very closely adapted to the particular ecosystem, being near the concrete realities of that place will be an absolute necessity for decision making.

Local control means more people on the land. It is absolutely unprecedented in the history of the world that 3 percent of the population should feed all the rest, as is now the case in many developed countries. Eighty percent of China's huge population is involved in food production. Our system may be incredible in terms of man-hour efficiency, but it is also, for that very reason, a precarious system. That pyramid of stability envisioned by Thomas Jefferson—a population base of many small independent landholders—has been flipped onto its tip. The table shows a likely pattern of employment shifts in our population as the new paradigm unfolds, as predicted by William Irwin Thompson.

DISTRIBUTION OF EMPLOYMENT OF U.S. POPULATION[7]

Sector	*1972*	*2000*
Agriculture	4%	40%
Industry	32%	20%
Services	64%	40%

The foods we choose to eat have a great deal to do with how we farm. One tendency that is in accord with new paradigm thinking and is becoming increasingly evident is a shift away from animal products, especially red meat. This change in diet has occurred for reasons of health and consciousness, for reasons of efficiency in food production, and for reasons of sensitivity to animals, especially in response to current confinement approaches to livestock production.

In the mid-1940s, we turned our war-honed technology (and consciousness) toward the land. Those first years of chemical-intensive farming led to a great boom in production. The question was then, as throughout the history of American agriculture, what are we to do with it all? Could we limit production—an aspect of voluntary simplicity—or could we find a way to consume this new excess? We found a way to consume. The answer was to increase the amount of red meat in our diets. To produce one pound of well-marbled red meat requires somewhere between five and twenty pounds of feed grain, depending upon the animal being fed and other variables. This was a way of getting people to pay for excess production. It was our chosen path, and now half of all cropland production is fed to animals, 90 percent of our corn, barley and oats, *more* than 90 percent of our soybeans.[8]

Wes Jackson has called this our cow and pig welfare program. It amounts to an enormous lot of make-work activity at the expense of our topsoil, global petroleum reserves, and, very likely, our health. If we were to suddenly eliminate grain-fed red meat from our diets, we would need only a fraction of the farmland we now plow. But the structure of much of American agriculture, if not the whole economy, would fall to pieces. Seemingly small cultural shifts may have enormous consequences in interconnected systems.

Meanwhile, half a billion human inhabitants of our planet are malnourished, many to the point of starvation. These, of course, are people here and throughout the world who cannot afford to pay for our excess production. (Because of our technological approach, with its dependence on increasingly expensive machines and chemicals, many expect this excess also to become increasingly expensive.) It should be noted here too that, in most cases, the food-producing abilities and population sizes of Third World countries were originally disrupted by factory-model influences of Western countries. I am talking here about such diverse factors as the Green Revolution, economic imperialism, and the effects of Western medicine, the blessings of all of which have been very mixed.

Our projected shift toward spiritual values would not, of course, sustain a system that feeds U.S. overproduction to confined animals while human populations starve. If, in fact, we continue to reduce our consumption of red meat, enormous amounts of food will be freed for hungry people. At the same time, marginal lands could be allowed to return to more beautiful and stable expressions of the ecosystem.

The problems of overproduction and of getting food to the world's hungry will provide a great challenge to the new system, should it in fact emerge. Surely, however, necessary adjustments are more likely to be accomplished in a system modeled on harmonious interconnectedness than in one based on competition. Finally, of course, it is far more important that we help other countries become self-sufficient in food than that we feed them our own overproduction.

It is only fair to mention here that many farmers argue that recently poor livestock markets have led to bad care of the land: millions of acres of pasture have been plowed for cash-producing, erosion-prone row crops. Many organic farmers, too, complain that without a livestock component in their operations they lose their source of manure for fertilizer, and the alfalfa crop which has been so important in their rotations becomes useless. Again, we can only suggest here that within the free energy and idea flow of a highly interconnected system, what is truly necessary for the health of that system should emerge.

A second food shift under way is the avoidance of chemically produced and processed foods. Sensitivity to the health of the environment and our bodies has lead to an increasing demand for whole and organic foods, even in the face of resistance by the food and medical establishments still operating within the old paradigm. A decision to move away from chemicals in farming would radically change agriculture. One farmer recently told me, for instance, that the size of our farms would have to be greatly reduced: "It was the need to cultivate that limited the size of our farms. Once we could control weeds with herbicides, we could farm all we could plant."

It is in just such a way that chemicals and technology have replaced people on the land.

We cannot deny that food in the United States has been cheap and abundant, and some argue that if we stop using chemicals, food costs for the consumer will rise. We argue the converse: that chemical companies have begun to price their products out of the market. Paul Gilk, writing in the *North Country Anvil,* has stated that "the organic future stubbornly asserts . . . that we should 'Become organic now and avoid the rush.' "[9]

In any case, if in fact the eco-model becomes the dominant factor, we can expect a great reduction in the use of—perhaps even abstinence from—chemicals. Pesticides and herbicides will be replaced by sensitivity to the growth cycles in plants and a precise awareness of the life cycles of insect pests and their predators to maintain an acceptable production balance. This eco-model approach to pests, usually described as integrated pest management, is a complex and demanding discipline that is continuously advancing. It assumes that the introduction of poisons into the system is the last strategy rather than the first.

Chemical fertilizers, in the new system, will be replaced by those fertility processes that originally developed our rich soils, that made them bloom and prosper even until this past generation. We are talking here of the waste of the living and the decay of the dead organisms. We in the West have been somewhat schizophrenic on this issue. Our attempts at forcing the world into the factory model have been in part a flight from the deep truth of the cycle of death, decay, and renewal. A shift to the eco-model would, of course, bring us back into a full relationship with this fundamental if, for many, painful truth.

Consequently, human "waste"—food that has passed through our bodies—will not continue to be wasted in increasingly expensive treatment plants while the land suffers for need of organic replenishing. Human waste will come to be considered, as it is now in the Orient, stored wealth of the ecosystem. First, however, we must stop mixing human waste with the chemical wastes from our daily lives, which makes it unsuitable for fertilizer. In time, the new paradigm thinker would argue, all such toxicity must be avoided, and our waste disposal become, in fact, a composting process, either on the community level or in our homes.

In that the "practical" approach of the old paradigm led to sterile disassociation from things so basic as human waste, it is interesting that the "high-flown" moral and spiritual course of the new paradigm leads us back to them. It can be expected that a shift to the systemic principles of the new model will lead to the healing of many such splits, which now fragment our lives and diminish the land.

NOTES

1. In Kenneth A. Hammond, George Marinko, and Wilma B. Fairchild, eds., *Sourcebook on the Environment* (Chicago: University of Chicago Press, 1978), p. 263.
2. In T. C. McLuhan, *Touch the Earth* (New York: Pocket Books, 1972), p. 56.
3. News release drawn from foreign agricultural service bulletin.
4. William Irwin Thompson, *Darkness and Scattered Light* (Garden City, NY: Anchor Books, 1977), p. 92.
5. The International Independence Institute, *The Community Land Trust: A Guide to a New Model for Land Tenure in America* (Cambridge, MA: Center for Community Economic Development, 1972), p. xiii.
6. Ibid., p. 1.
7. Thompson, p. 89.
8. Frances Moore Lappé, *Diet for a Small Planet* (New York: Ballantine Books, 1976), pp. 12, 13.
9. Paul Gilk, "Adapt or Die," *North Country Anvil*, Winter 1983–84, p. 11.

·14·

Ecoculture

IN this chapter we explore forms of agriculture that might provide stability for both the land and the human future. Some are adaptations of time-tested traditional approaches. Others reflect what might be considered a new vision. In the main, agriculture is being reenvisioned by scientists who, for whatever reasons, reject the industrial logic that has reduced food production to its current limited and dangerous dimensions. In their holistic point of view, production and profit are tempered by the demands of the spiritual, the ethical, and the aesthetic. What is most strong in each of them, it seems to us, is that the usual scientific fascination with the power of technology is far overshadowed by an intense interest in the workings of the ecosystem—a sort of practical reverence.

One step toward new agricultural stability might be a partial return to the farming that dominated the American landscape before World War II. That approach, which is now reemerging in thousands of organic farms, evolved from European agriculture and was brought to this continent by generations of immigrants. It is the style of agriculture—and of life—for which Wendell Berry has argued. It is our traditional agriculture, and practiced with mindful diligence, it can be sustained over long periods of time.

The key to the success of our traditional farm is tied to a diversity that allows it, in large part, to be self-sustaining. This farm produces a variety of crops, each providing complementary balance to the others. Some aid in weed control, others in maintaining the fertility of the soil. A given field is planted in a different crop each year. In the Midwest, for instance, the crop rotation in organic agriculture goes something like this: in successive years a field will be planted in corn, small grain, alfalfa, soybeans, and again corn. Marginal land is left in woodlot and pasture. Livestock has been a traditional part of this farm, both in the use of draught animals and for production of meat, eggs, and dairy products. The animals are fed from the farm's own fields, and animal manure, of course, is fundamental to its fertility program.

A man whose judgment I tend to respect said to me, in reference to this kind of farming, "When I look at today's organic farming approaches, I can't see anything different from the farm of the 1930s. Do we want to go back fifty years?"

Despite our current (old paradigm) fear of regressing, we just might gain a great deal by retreating a little at this point. After all, history is not a circle, but a spiral, and any return to the past cannot take away what has gone on in between. There is much that we have learned since the 1930s, and if something like the diverse organic farm of that period becomes once again our agricultural standard, it will, of course, express such new understanding. It is likely, too, that far more of the farming community will be aware of the highest possible standards for operating such a farm.

Should livestock not be so large a part of these new-old farms, operators will have to turn to composting and green manure—special plant crops such as Sudan grass which, when plowed back in, enrich the soil. As suggested earlier, perhaps, too, we will come to accept that we human beings are the "livestock" our fields support. Using human waste for fertilizer, we will thereby finally close what has been a serious break in the ecological cycle, the results of which have been polluting our streams and rivers for generations.

Within our traditional agriculture there is room for plenty of imaginative growth. Missouri farmer-scientist Eugene Poirot had the luck to inherit two 900-acre parcels of land. One was a worn-out farm, its fertility so low that "you couldn't get your seed back." The other was virgin prairie never touched by a plow. Few would have resisted the temptation to exploit the untouched land. Poirot, however, who had been influenced by soil scientist Dr. William Albrecht, chose not to break the virgin prairie; but to keep it intact as a model of good health in the land. Through study of natural fertility, he would restore his worn-out farm to original health. His book *Our Margin of Life* expresses his philosophy and describes that restorative adventure: "Instruction for restoration based on . . . sciences may be simply given by saying 'return that which has been taken and hold the soil in place.'"[1]

Anyone who has seen the movie made of Poirot's farming operation knows that technology is not his first love. I have heard audiences of farmers laugh at the machinery with which he "made do." They found his planting corn directly into well-established sods equally humorous. Production figures that put his "worn-out" farm among the top 5 percent in the country, including 200-plus bushels of corn per acre, were, however, less laughable. In the main, healthy soil, not industrial inputs, was the key to this success.

Though his methods were scientific, Poirot's guides were the natural prairie and the health of his crops and that of the wildlife and livestock they supported. With its brushy margins, its creek, and catfish and irrigation ponds, this farm didn't seem much like a farm at all. In his book Poirot expresses a love for wildlife that equals his love for farming. Indeed, it reveals these to be part of a single continuum.

Under the influence of the eco-model, it is very possible that our agriculture will move, at least in part, to even smaller and more complexly interconnected operations. Richard Merrill, in his essay "Toward a Self-sustaining Agriculture," writes that one model for production would be:

> the rice-vegetable-fish-livestock economies of southern and eastern Asia. Adapted to current information about ecological principles and a holistic science, modern polyculture farms would link several artificial ecosystems in a balanced and relatively self-sufficient complex of renewable energy systems, mixed crops, aquaculture, plus livestock and insect husbandry. At present, several grassroots groups in America and Europe are investigating various ways to integrate renewable food and energy systems into endemic polyculture schemes.[2]

In these smaller farms, aquaculture becomes an integral part of the overall system. In suitable climates, rice is a staple crop. Other pond-vegetable crops, such as protein-rich algae, are a possibility. In the very healthy dietary system that corresponds with this approach to farming, fish, along with poultry and beans, provides the primary sources of protein. The pond, then, is managed so as to produce an abundance of fast-growing, palatable food fish of several varieties, each with a particular ecological niche within the pond. Fishes commonly raised include catfish, trout, talapia, carp, perch, bullhead, and bluegills.

In recent years, as the cattle market has waned, fish production in this country has grown tremendously, especially catfish and trout. But here, as with other cash crops, the factory model has controlled the approach. Fish are fed commercially prepared chows, and chemicals are a part of pond maintenance. In *Hard Tomatoes, Hard Times,* Jim Hightower writes that fish producers have even begun to skin their fish chemically.

In the Oriental and eco-model approach, on the other hand, weed growth in ponds is controlled by human labor or through rotation of crops. Fish are fed by organically fertilizing the water to stimulate food growth, by attracting insects to the pond, or by culturing such fish foods as earthworms and midges.

The operators of such intensive polyculture farms would be in far less hurry to send soil-laden spring and heavy rain runoffs racing through tiles, down ditches, and into channelized streams to flood our major rivers, only to see late-season drought wither our crops. Seldom, in the dog days of late summer, do we have that optimum of water necessary for peak crop production. The multi-use erosion and flood-control catch pond—wherever there is runoff and a suitable low spot—becomes a major resource of the small poly farm. Crops can then be irrigated with water enriched by fish manure, and the water moved to the fields by gravity, windmills, or methane-driven pumps. Every five to ten years, ponds can be drained and rich bottom residues spread as fertilizer on surrounding fields and gardens.

New Alchemy, on Cape Cod in Massachusetts, has been the site of experimentation for even more concentrated approaches to food production. Two of its originators, Nancy Jack Todd and John Todd, in their book *Bioshelters, Ocean Arks, City Farming: Ecology as the Basis of Design,* list nine precepts they have followed in designing their polycultural food-producing and living systems. These precepts are illuminating.

1. The living world is the matrix of all design.
2. Design should follow, not oppose, the laws of life.
3. Biological equity must determine design.
4. Design must reflect bioregionality.
5. Projects should be based on renewable energy resources.
6. Design should be sustainable through the integration of living systems.
7. Design should be coevolutionary with the natural world.
8. Building and design should help heal the planet.
9. Design should follow a sacred ecology.[3]

Food production at New Alchemy falls into two general categories. One involves organic vegetable gardens and tree crops that provide fruit and nuts, lumber, fuel, and food for livestock. The other has concentrated on the culture of fish and aquatic animals. Much of this work is housed in "bioshelters," which are a marriage in design between biology and architecture. Interestingly, the people of New Alchemy found inspiration in a centuries-old traditional Indonesian farm in Java:

> There was a farm, one of many that had been farmed continuously for centuries, which reflected in miniature the major restorative processes in nature. Whereas most agriculture as a rule is short lived, lasting a few centuries at the most before the land tires and falls into disrepair, this was a farm where fertility was probably increasing each year as it had for hundreds of years—an example of a true partnership between the people and the land. All the major types of agriculture had been interwoven and balanced on one piece of land. There were trees, livestock, grains, grasses, vegetables, and fishes, but no single one of these was allowed to dominate. As significant as the disparate elements were the connecting relationships between the water/aquaculture, and land/agriculture. We in the West almost never

join water and land this way, which may explain partially why our efforts in agriculture are relatively short lived. The Java farm was hilly. Although the native forest was gone, it had been replaced by a domestic forest of trees with economic and food value which protected the hillsides, farm houses and buildings, as well as the crops and fish culture below.

Water entered the farm in a relatively pure state via an aqueduct or ditch along the contour of the land. To charge it with nutrients so that it would fertilize as well as irrigate the crops, the aqueduct passed directly under the animal sheds and the household latrine. The manure-enriched water was subsequently aerated by passing over a small waterfall. It then flowed between the deep channels between the crops in raised beds where it did not splash directly onto the crops, but seeped laterally into the beds. In this way animal and human wastes were used but contamination of crops by pathogens harmful to animals or humans was minimized.

The gardens thus filtered and, to a degree, purified the water. Water neither absorbed nor lost to the garden then formed a channel where it flowed into small ponds in which fish, which require water high in nutrients, were hatched and raised. The banks of the aquaculture ponds were planted with a variety of tuberous plants. The leaves were fed to the fish and the tubers to the livestock.

The water, enriched by the fish for a second time, then flowed into rice paddies, flooding and fertilizing them. The nutrient and purification cycle was repeated. The rice filtered out the nutrients and the organic materials and the water left the paddy in a purer state. At the bottom reaches of the farm, the water entered a large communal, partially managed, pond. From time to time organic matter, including sediments, was taken from the pond and carted up to fertilize the soils on the higher reaches of the landscape.

On this Java farm integration was maximized. What was most interesting was the exacting degree to which the farmers had worked out the relationships with the patterns of balanced interdependence between the var-

> ious components. Had pesticides been applied, for example, the fish being highly sensitive to toxins would have died and the chain of ecological relationships would have broken. . . . In more remote areas of Java, where Western ways have less impact, there is still a high level of cultural integration as well. Art and religion are as much a part of daily life as the tending of plants and animals. The sacred and the aesthetic have not been fragmented and diverted off in separate directions as is the case with much of our spiritual and artistic forms.[4]

In an effort to control erosion, many U.S. farmers have recently turned away from the traditional moldboard plow. They are instead chisel plowing, disking, ridge-tilling, and no-tilling. New paradigm agricultural thinkers are attracted to the idea of no tillage at all. A Japanese farmer, Masanobu Fukuoka, perfected such a system on his tiny farm in southern Japan and has written a now famous book about it, *The One-Straw Revolution.* What is hoped is that the forces of nature, as natural process, can be guided to grow the things we need. That is, in larger and larger part, nature will do the growing, humanity will harvest. Rather than agriculture, such an approach might better be termed *ecoculture.*

In this country, Wes Jackson and others at the Land Institute in Salina, Kansas, are working along lines in part similar to those of Fukuoka, but having far greater implications. According to Jackson, till agriculture, plowing up the ground, has never really been compatible with a healthy environment. The realities of such farming, which must include human ethical limitations, have almost always led to destruction of the soil. "The plowshare," states Jackson, "has destroyed more options for the future than has the sword." Our problem as agriculturalists, he suggests, is that at heart we are still hunters and gatherers. So little of our history has been spent behind the plow, and we balk at the intrusive demands of good farming.

Jackson wonders if we might not develop an agriculture "more moral than we are," so that it is possible for us to "sin without damaging the earth." What he envisions, he admits, is far in the future, but he is working toward a mixed prairie permaculture of perennial food plants. This would mean a crop-producing prairie ecosystem that might need to be reseeded only every three or four years—perhaps, in time, considerably less often. Despite some scientific doubt about the productive capability of perennial plants, the Land Institute is now experimenting with numerous prairie perennials that do indeed show promise of producing acceptable yields. To what degree these permacultures will have to be tended is perhaps not yet clear. In any case, the complex root systems of such a permaculture will hold down the soil, and the fertility of that soil will increase much as it did under the virgin prairie.

In his *New Roots for Agriculture,* Jackson expands on this idea of the self-sustaining prairie:

> In a successful herbaceous perennial polyculture, we would expect that soil erosion would cease to be a problem. Because of the chemical diversity of such an ecosystem, insects and plant diseases would also be less serious. In a natural prairie polyculture, weeds are managed by the shading system. Nutrient balance is also managed by the system with little human involvement. Water is held by the spongy mass and a deeply penetrating root system has a wick effect and "pulls" water down when the heavy rains occur. Once a balanced polyculture has been planted, soil preparation and preparation of seed and planting are all done by the system.[5]

Under such a system, costs for seed and fossil fuels will, of course, be enormously reduced. As with New Alchemy, the vision of those at the Land Institute reaches well beyond the biological aspects of establishing its permacultures to include social and spiritual ones as well.

Back in 1950, J. Russell Smith published a book entitled *Tree Crops,* which envisioned another form of soil-saving permaculture. Though not based in currently preferred foods, this permaculture may, technically at least, be far less difficult to establish than a food-producing prairie permaculture. Smith found examples of populations in Mediterranean Europe that had for centuries made much of their living from tree crops.

Smith argues that plow agriculture and its specific crops were meant for flat land, but that we have, with disastrous results, brought them to the hills. Tree crops, he believes, would solve our erosion problem and beautify our landscape. He contrasts agriculturally created deserts with the "comparative Edens" of tree-crop areas such as the chestnut forests of Corsica, and provides evidence that tree crops produce an abundance of food. In the main, as he sees it, this food would be fed to livestock animals, which now eat most of our grain production. He is enthusiastic about the abundance of food even wild varieties of trees produce:

> A single oak tree yields acorns (good carbohydrate food) often by the hundredweight, sometimes by the ton. Some hickory and pecan trees give us nuts by the barrel; the walnut tree yields by the ten bushels. There are bean trees producing good food for cattle, which food would apparently make more meat or milk per acre than our forage crops now make. It is even now probable that the king of all forage crops is a Hawaiian bean tree, the keawe.[6]

Smith argues that through tree crops we could double the area of cropland in the United States and in so doing solve much of our erosion problem. Beyond their capacity to thrive on "marginal" lands, trees are also more drought-resistant than annual crops and, in terms of experimental breeding, hold a great advantage over most annuals:

> We propagate trees by twig or bud, by grafting or budding. Therefore, any wild, unstable (though useful) freak, any helpless malformation like the navel orange which cannot reproduce itself, can be made into a million trees by the nurseryman. The parent tree of the Red Delicious variety of apple grew, by chance, in an Iowa fence row. A representative of the Stark Nursery Company saw the apple at a fair and raced with all speed to the tree, bought it, and reproduced it by the million.[7]

The great problem with tree crops, one must suppose, is how long it takes to establish crop-producing orchards or forests. In a relatively new nation such as ours, in the habit of instant gratification, the planting of trees may not be a welcome proposal. We find it hard enough to make it from season to season; to plant what we ourselves may never harvest requires a generosity and vision that may be unattainable. With these limitations in mind, the planting of tree crops might have a greater chance of success in the public than the private sector.

The concept of permacultures of food plants, which could help us to reclaim lands that have become barren, is an exciting new area in food production. Rosemary Menninger, in the *Next Whole Earth Catalog,* writes: "Permaculture describes perennial-based low-maintenance gardening and farming. . . . [It] goes hand in hand with the Japanese edible wilderness gardening technique described in . . . [Fukuoka's] *One-Straw Revolution.* . . . Together they conjure up the first whole-systems approach to agriculture, allowing nature to do most of the work and humans to do most of the harvesting."[8]

Menninger quotes from *Permaculture One,* by Bill Mollison and David Holmgren of Australia, where permaculture is being studied intensively:

> You can construct, using these plants, a series of forests in which you start underground with tuberous species and with rhizomes and also there's a huge variety of fungi which live in the mulch leaf litter. You can come up, through short perennial herbs, through taller herbs, small bushes, small woody plants, medium-sized woody plants and so on up, and create, not so much a three-tier agriculture as a multi-tier agriculture which then forms a sort of closed jungle system. If you stand off from that you can often see a place in it where you can put yet more species. For instance, even in a quite closed system, vines will emerge and thrive."[9]

Such intensive techniques remind us that there are those who believe that the ultimate in food production and life-style is not farming, but gardening. For them the garden is a place of wonder, of enlightenment. What they mean, perhaps, is that we should return to *the* garden. The reductive factory-model approach to our world was, as they see it, *the fall.* The biodynamic gardeners of Europe who live according to the philosophical teachings of Rudolph Steiner may be said to follow such a path, finding gardening a deeply spiritual discipline. Other gardeners have adopted the magical and prayerful approaches that distinguish the gardens of Findhorn in Scotland.

In discussing any form of agriculture, one must not forget the seeds from which our food plants grow. In them is concentrated the genetic wisdom of the ages. As is increasingly clear, Western agriculture has concentrated its food production into too few varieties of seed. These are hybrids, developed to provide high yields in the artificial conditions of the modern factory farm. They depend on chemical fertilizers, pesticides, and, in dry climates, irrigation. The farmer who uses these seeds must have plenty of money or the system will surely fail.

Meanwhile, the great genetic diversity of our agricultural heritage has been ignored or even, in many instances, lost. Ecological wisdom suggests that such losses have weakened our connection with life. Using a single variety of plant means, for instance, that a single disease to which it is not resistant could do enormous damage to that crop, even on a nationwide scale. We have already seen how the ecosystem responded to our concentrated use of the American elm as our shade tree. Since the onset of Dutch elm disease, we have thousands of barren city streets to remind us of the potential for death inherent in monoculture. In 1970, corn blight struck a broad area of the southern United States where most farmers had planted a single variety of unresistant corn. It is clear that we must not trust our food future to a single basket of seed.

An ecological agriculture will honor the great genetic diversity of our natural and agricultural heritage. We will carefully save seeds from all varieties that have come to us from the past. We will also, for any given bioregion, use seeds that have adapted to it over many generations, even centuries, of plant life. To the extent that we do aid in the evolution of our food plants, we will again concentrate on their adaptation to the natural conditions of a specific region. Our continuing destruction of natural ecosystems and the genetic diversity they contain carries with it costs to the future that most of us can but dimly imagine.

In the southwestern United States, a young researcher named Gary Nabhan has been working with the Southwest Crop Conservancy Garden and Seed Bank to save the seeds and techniques of the region's traditional Indian agriculture. Rather than force the entire desert to bloom, at whatever cost in water and fossil fuels, Nabhan suggests we concentrate desert agriculture on moisture- and nutrient-rich floodplains. He also suggests that we develop new agricultural plants from native ones and that we mimic their techniques for survival.[10] In a region where the costs of irrigation have made the production of conventional food plants increasingly marginal, Nabhan and his coworkers have brought to light ancient varieties of corn, beans, melons, and other food plants that thrive on as little as five inches of rain per year and in temperatures of up to 120 degrees.[11]

In the future, even our architecture may express new approaches to food production. In *Darkness and Scattered Light,* William Irwin Thompson writes of houses that will provide the food and energy for those who live in them. Our houses, then, may become increasingly sophisticated solar collectors with substantial greenhouses and fish tanks. The component parts, like cells with semipermeable membranes, will allow "information" (energy, light, nutrients) to pass through them, while maintaining, at the same time, their individual integrity. Some of their finest living space may be *one* with production space. All residues and wastes would, of course, be composted or in other ways recycled through the omni-directional system that would be the harmony of such a living space. We already have numerous first models for "the integral urban house." And even more numerous one- and two-acre self-sufficiency systems have begun to spring up here and there around the countryside.

If we renounce our current factory-model agriculture, proponents of the deep ecology perspective believe that to some extent we can return to simple harvesting—perhaps in more sophisticated ways—of pure nature. It is estimated that, even now, some 200 million people around the world are still to some degree hunters and gatherers. To return to this approach in any significant way we could not insist on our traditional European food plants; we would have to adapt to the nutrition nature provides. Certainly there are wild greens in abundance, and there are natural ecosystem monocultures such as the wild rice stands and cattail marshes of the north.

For those who continue to eat red meat, certain stretches of our Great Plains (or those, say, of Africa and Asia) might be managed for "wild livestock," much as moose herds are now managed in Alaska. Our Great Plains once carried sixty million buffalo, and about as many antelope. These numbers rival our current production of beef cattle over the same area. Perhaps here and there, we could allow some portion of that old greatness to emerge again with the grass, collectively herded and harvested. Our largest obstacle here might be our inability to accept the necessary communal form of land "ownership," but such an approach truly would be the mirror opposite of our contemporary feedlot confinement operations.

Probably most Americans would be surprised to see very much of what we have conjectured about here come to fruition in the near future—say, by the year 2010. Yet most new paradigm thinkers would be even more surprised if our contemporary factory-model food production were to continue till that time. If high technology, with its supercomputer, proves after all to be the key to our agricultural future, we can expect that it, too, will have had to adapt to the wisdom inherent in the eco-model.

Many who take an economic approach to change argue that the same market forces that led us into contemporary agriculture will lead us into the alternative approaches described in this chapter. Others argue that what we need most, if these changes are to come about, are programs that will bring more and more people back to the land. With the tremendous imbalance between food-producers and urban consumers, however, it seems more likely that some cultural breakdown, rather than government programs, will accomplish such a resettling of the land.

Much of what we have described here has already begun. And change is always in process. Aging, decay, renewal. Yet if the new paradigm eco-model that is the basis for these approaches to agriculture *takes,* if it *is* the truth for our time, if it has the capacity to solve our problems—and we are worthy—the concrete reality will emerge as inevitably as apples swell from spring blossoms or the sun rises in the morning to release itself into the life of the planet.

Soil, as we wrote at the outset, is the stuff of our flesh and our future. Even what remains is immense with possibility for the continuance of life. The life in the soil, as we are told, is greater in mass than that which exists above ground. What has been lost amounts to greater slaughter than that of the buffalo and the passenger pigeon. But that which remains can and will continue to work for us; those "twelve underground horses per acre," like those real ones that brought farmers home through the blinding dust storms of the thirties, will pull for us even yet. To aid us in our survival, they require neither more nor less than their own.

NOTES

1. Eugene M. Poirot, *Our Margin of Life* (Raytown, MO: Acres U.S.A., 1978), p. 62.
2. Richard Merrill, *Radical Agriculture* (New York: Harper Colophon Books, 1976), p. 318.
3. Nancy Jack Todd and John Todd, *Bioshelters, Ocean Arks, City Farming: Ecology as the Basis of Design* (San Francisco: Sierra Club Books, 1984), table of contents.Copyright 1984 by the authors. Reprinted by permission of Sierra Club Books.
4. Ibid., pp. 67–68.
5. Wes Jackson, *New Roots for Agriculture* (Lincoln: University of Nebraska Press, 1985).
6. J. Russell Smith, *Tree Crops* (New York: Devin-Adair, 1950), pp. 12, 13.
7. Ibid., p. 16.
8. Rosemary Menninger, review of *Permaculture One* and *Permaculture Two, The Next Whole Earth Catalog* 1980, p. 83.
9. Ibid.
10. Gary Paul Nabhan, "Replenishing Desert Agriculture with Native Plants and Their Symbionts," in Wes Jackson, Wendell Berry, Bruce Colman, eds., *Meeting the Expectations of the Land* (Berkeley, CA: North Point Press, 1984), pp. 174–181.
11. Noel Vietmeyer, "Saving the Beauty of a Harsh and Meager Land," *Audubon*, January 1985, p. 100–106.

· 15 ·

Epilogue:

YOU ARE ALREADY INVOLVED

MANY of us today feel that we, our institutions, and our environment need help. And most of us feel, at least every now and then, that we want to give help, but the causes often seem distant, our possible influence small. The vanishing whales, the "greenhouse effect," nuclear destruction—these perils seem overwhelming. Contemplating them, we feel hopeless.

But most of us live near food-producing land, and most of this land is being threatened in numerous ways. We do not want to urge anyone to ignore distant issues, but we also have a serious problem right in our own backyards, one whose dimension and solution justify taking direct personal responsibility. We suggest that you consider making the preservation of your local farmland a personal cause. Surely others in your community would also like to do good work for the future of our planet. Together you can work toward preservation of our precious farmland. If you are already part of such a group, we suggest that you and the other members explore land stewardship.

Along what lines you will work will be up to you and/or your group, but the following two sections of this chapter, based on the experience of the Land Stewardship Project of St. Paul, Minnesota, will offer some specific suggestions. The first section describes an effective awareness and planning meeting. The second suggests courses of action committed individuals or groups might follow. After the first few steps, the path becomes clear.

The First Meeting

The land stewardship meeting brings together a group of interested, perhaps even concerned people. It should articulate and clarify what these people already know about farmland conservation and its problems in their area. It should also *extend* what they know about these issues. The participants should visualize what they consider an ideal future for local farmland, and they should develop a tentative plan of action to achieve such a future.

It might be helpful for you to consider what the Land Stewardship Project describes as its four basic assumptions:

1. The diminishment of our farmland through erosion, development, and poor farming practices is a serious and continuing problem.
2. This is not just the problem of farmers.
3. This is not an unsolved technical problem.
4. The source of our failure to solve the problem, therefore, must lie in our unwillingness to commit ourselves and our resources to dealing with it.

These four assumptions should be spelled out and documented. In terms of the first assumption, that there is a problem, you should have relevant statistics, examples, and perhaps photographs or slides on hand. Your local library and Soil Conservation Service will quickly provide you with more of this information than you can possibly use. Though it is important that you set the problem in its larger contexts, it is even more important that the local circumstances be made clear. Here, especially, local Soil Conservation Service information will be useful to you. We also invite you to contact the Land Stewardship Project at 512 Elm, Stillwater, Minnesota 55082, for helpful information.

In discussing the assumption that the problem is not just that of farmers, everyone must understand that less than 3 percent of our population provides food for all the rest of us. City dwellers, especially children, scarcely know how food gets into supermarkets. Everyone must realize that we all are sustained by farmland and that farmers—in the traditional, not the corporate sense of the word—need the political, financial, and moral support of those for whom they grow food. We should also insist on high-quality food and care for the land.

In arguing for our third premise, that good farmland conservation is not an unsolved technological problem, it is useful to have an expert on hand—unless, of course, you are an expert. Otherwise, you might ask an employee of your local Soil Conservation Service or a conservation farmer. In rural areas, it is common for a dozen or more such experts to be present at a land stewardship meeting. These specialists can describe farm conservation techniques such as terraces, grassed waterways, shelterbelts, and conservation tillage. In the words of conservation farmer Milo Hanson: "On the technical side, we know how. You bet we know how to conserve soil and water. Of course, we are always trying to improve. We are always learning. But we have enough knowledge to stop soil erosion to a high degree, so there would be very, very little erosion. If we really did what we know we should do."[1]

Finally, if we accept the fact that there is a problem and that we know how to solve it, but haven't done so, then we must also concede that the fault lies in our societal and individual selfishness and avoidance. Some in your audience will surely try to blame our financial limitations instead, but, as we have argued, the necessary allocation of money will follow only upon correct attitudes, both individual and societal.

Admittedly, some individual farmers could not afford to implement complete conservation plans on their land overnight. But, with public support and conservation costs included in the price of food, we, as a society, could easily afford to care for our land. For that matter, no one has ever claimed destruction of farmland to be good economics.

Because we regard the source of our farmland problems as neither technical nor financial, but *human,* we feel it is important for as many people as possible to be involved. We can all help to spread awareness of the issue. We can all help to intensify societal commitment to solving the problem.

If you think it would be useful to show an appropriate movie, many are available from the Soil Conservation Service, the extension service, or the agricultural schools in your area.

After there is some understanding reached as to the four assumptions, group members might begin to envision what they consider to be an ideal future for local farmland. It may be good to have a little quiet time, so that each can make a specific list. It may be even better to break up into small groups to accomplish this. The final list should be posted where everyone can see it, and copies may later be mailed to each participant.

Once the ideal has been defined, the same procedures should be followed to develop a plan of action. The material in the next section will offer some specific suggestions for action to help preserve your local farmland.

Local Action

The Land Stewardship Project has found that after these initial meetings, local or county committees have been very effective in promoting sound farmland conservation. They have demonstrated what concerned citizens can do. With luck, your initial meeting will attract a core of people with enthusiasm for the land stewardship issue. Most likely some of them will be farmers, clergy, teachers, conservation professionals, and others whose work can contribute to the goals of the committee. You should, in fact, try to widen your membership to include people whose community roles affect public policy, such as county commissioners, soil supervisors, and journalists. Support from people in these key positions will add greatly to your clout.

You must also, of course, work closely with local Soil Conservation Service personnel, extension agents, and environmental groups already involved in soil conservation. Service and sportsmen's clubs, women's groups, and church groups may also want to support your goals. A network of concerned citizens will help to spread the message throughout your area and will lend credibility to the cause.

The Land Stewardship Project has supported many such action committees in a five-state area of the upper Midwest. These committees have identified local problems and brought them to the public eye. They have also made concrete efforts to correct them. In Minnesota, the Winona County Project was developed to provide a model for local land stewardship efforts. The following examples of that model committee's accomplishments may prove useful in guiding the efforts of your own:

1. *Development of a Community Garden in the City of Winona.* A local church donated the extended use of a plot of land, and volunteers of all ages have planted a garden that provides low-cost, high-quality food to area residents and a local food shelf. Work on this project has taught volunteers the techniques of organic gardening and the advantages of a local food supply. Seeds, plants, and machinery are provided by local nurseries and implement dealers. Protected by a shelterbelt of trees planted by volunteers, this garden provides an example of how a community can work harmoniously with the land.

2. *Township Meetings for Farmers.* Working closely with the Soil Conservation Service, the committee invites local farmers to meetings in each township of the county. The findings of township soil surveys are presented, and aerial photographs are shown. The conservation needs of specific fields are pointed out. Farmers thus see clearly the effects erosion has had on their land and are told how to correct them. Many sign cooperator's agreements with the SCS directly after the meetings.

3. *Educational Programs.* The committee has several educational programs directed at people in various age groups and professions:

a. Workshops that show elementary teachers materials and activities that spotlight aspects of soil erosion and the need for conservation.

b. Exhibits at county and agricultural fairs that show such things as the differing effects of rainfall upon protected and unprotected soil. In one case a dump truck containing ten tons of soil was parked near the display. A nearby sign told passers-by that this was the average yearly amount of soil lost per acre on area farms.

c. Tours of conservation farms for area clergy and the general public. Information and materials are provided to those who take the tours.

4. *Tree Plantings.* Committee members have obtained grants to purchase trees for planting shelterbelts on public and private land. Classes of elementary students, Boy Scouts, Girl Scouts, and other groups are taught the purpose of shelterbelts and are supervised in their planting work by local foresters. Activities such as this, when well publicized, help to educate the community as well as to actually protect land.

5. *Awards.* The committee periodically awards certificates of recognition to good stewards of the land. A local newspaper prints interviews with recipients as a monthly feature. Other area papers reprint them. Such awards convey to the public the importance of good land stewardship and reward those who have practiced it. A yearly conservation prize is awarded to the best 4-H conservation project. One recent winner received, as prize, a plane ride over the county's agricultural land.

6. *Peer Pressure.* Some of the most dramatic accomplishments have been achieved by confronting land owners and operators whose methods had been damaging the land. Often those confronted owners were absentee owners unaware of the practices of their operators. With soil losses amounting to twenty or thirty tons per acre per year, many owners have been only too willing to protect their investment with conservation practices.

7. *Corporate Responsibility.* The committee is looking into the care of land foreclosed upon by large corporations such as insurance companies. In one instance, members met with representatives of a company whose land assets were valued at more than two billion dollars. Committee members argued, with some success, for changes in farming practices and the development of a company stewardship policy. The national news coverage received in this instance underlined the need for corporate responsibility for farmland.

8. *Covenants.* The committee is exploring model farmland leases and sales contracts incorporating soil conservation covenants that will prevent new owners from destroying conservation practices already in place.

9. *Political Action.* Based on the concept that stewardship, like farming itself, is everyone's concern, committee members closely monitor and attempt to influence local land-use legislation. They attend local board meetings and press for adoption of soil-loss-limits regulations, farmland planning and zoning ordinances, and water-quality policies. Such political action helps to create a political and legal environment within which good stewardship can exist.

Citizen action has become an effective tool for change in the United States in the twentieth century. It has passed laws, altered policy, stopped wars, and ousted corrupt officials. It does so by creating a constituency for change, a consensus that cannot be denied. Dust storms and the work of soil conservationists such as Hugh Hammond Bennett created the consensus that led to the formation of the Soil Erosion Service in the 1930s. We must again create such a consensus if our soil is to be protected.

"Think globally and act locally" is a particularly apt slogan for soil conservation. As global as is our current erosion problem, it is also the most local of issues. Each of us has the earth under his or her feet, and ultimately, all of the physical work of soil conservation must be done locally. Any conservation work, however limited, helps solve the problem. One hillside protected by a terrace, one field sheltered from the winter winds, one farmer converted, one community-wide soil conservation plan—each of these actually saves some of the soil upon which the future of life depends.

We have long been waiting for government to pass legislation that will confront erosion and other farmland problems. We have repeatedly been disappointed. This need not stop us. While we work for protective legislation, we must plant trees and build a consensus so that, finally, government will have no choice but to provide the legislation necessary to preserve the land.

NOTES

1. Joe Paddock, from unpublished transcript of interview with Milo Hanson of Lac Qui Parle County, MN, 1984.

Index